T0129307

Grief, Spirit, Love, Joy

Paula De Francesca

BALBOA.
PRESS

A DIVISION OF HAY HOUSE

Balboa Press books may be ordered through booksellers or by contacting:

Balboa Press
A Division of Hay House
1663 Liberty Drive
Bloomington, IN 47403
www.balboapress.com.au
1 (877) 407-4847

Print information available on the last page.

ISBN: 978-1-5043-1918-8 (sc)
ISBN: 978-1-5043-1919-5 (e)

Balboa Press rev. date: 08/29/2019

May we all be connected with one another here on earth and in spirit form, and may love and kindness continue to connect us all.

The experience of grief can push us forward to awaken our spirituality.

Where we may feel there is emptiness, there is always faith surrounding us. We are not alone.

Here on Earth

Each spirit has a role to fulfil. When I chose this life, I acknowledged that everything I needed was being provided to help and guide me on this, my life path.

When I came into this world, I chose parents who were in their thirties, along with two older siblings. My brother was twelve years older and my sister nine years older than I was.

The story around my birth is that Mum wanted to have another baby, but Dad said, "We have just got our sleep routine back." But off they went to a party, got a bit tipsy, and a few months later found out I was on my way.

I learnt my first lesson around karma in the story my mum loves sharing with me. Her best friend had three children. Her eldest was my brother's age, and she had two girls, and she had just found out that she was pregnant again. My mum had laughed at her—and then found herself in the same situation. It was karma! This was the seventies, so to be pregnant in their late thirties was also seen as taboo.

My parents were always quick to say that I was their best present ever, a true gift. I did feel this as I was cuddled and welcomed.

Of course, I know now that we pick our parents for the lessons we need. They become part of our soul families.

My grandmother called me a *zingara*, which means "gypsy" in Italian. Wherever my family went, I was brought along for the ride.

Being a quiet child, I was happy to just sit at the table and listen to adults talking. I was subjected to topics including politics and happenings in various families. My grandmother had weekly Tuesday catch-ups with her friends, and I was included.

It wasn't unusual to come home from school and find Mum having a cup of tea and cake with one or two of the lovely neighbours we had. My mum was like the glue for the neighbourhood, bringing together all nationalities, fostering friendships, and always looking for the good in each person.

As my siblings were older, I often felt like an only child. School holidays and after school hours were spent helping my parents, reading, or playing imaginative games.

I was very close to my grandmother, who only lived three houses down. If I didn't like what Mum was making for dinner, I wandered down to see my grandmother, Nonna Maria.

I always accompanied Nonna Maria to church on Sunday mornings. My grandfather drove us in his car, and as he was unable to change the gears smoothly, we bunny-hopped down the road. And my grandmother, even though she couldn't drive, offered directions and instructions. We usually stopped and picked up some of my grandparents' friends along the way. I especially loved the 9:00 a.m. Italian Mass. The prayers seemed so much deeper in this language.

I would come home from church and set up my stuffed animal collection, including a dog, panda, and a clown. I provided them with a sermon, a teaching of what the priest had spoken about.

Throughout high school, I entertained the thought of becoming a missionary. When I was in Italy in my late teens, I visited a convent. But I also always wanted to be a wife and mother.

I was always quiet at school. On every report card the teachers wrote, "Paula is very bright, but we would love to hear her voice." I didn't get into the school choir for that exact reason. I couldn't be heard.

At home, I loved to stand at my blackboard and teach. I used my dog, Raegan, as my student. Raegan was a beautiful cocker spaniel. Abandoned by her previous owner, she chose me to follow home from school one day, and she became part of our family. Being quite shy, I was content to teach imaginary people or pets.

I had a very vivid imagination and loved to write stories and poems. I could see the story in my head and then see it play out. I also loved reading, and I consumed book after book. When I started high school, I clung to the first person I met. At recess and lunch, for a full year, we just read or went to the library. I was particularly fond of romance novels, where there were happy endings and the authors always looked for the good in situations. I also enjoyed biographies.

I still have an amazing thirst for knowledge and human stories. I want to know answers to questions. Why does this happen? Why do people think and react that way? I love hearing people's stories and the way they got to specific points in their lives. When I ask someone, "How are you?" I really am interested in the person's response and well-being.

When I was a child, our family always had music playing. We went to dinner dances, where everyone danced to various bands. On Saturday afternoons, we all came together to listen to records and dance around the living room. Some weekends my brother and his band jammed in the garage.

I found myself drawn to music too; certain songs resonated very deeply. I went to a fashion show with my mum, and two songs that were played were "There Must Be an Angel," by the Eurythmics, and "Walking on Sunshine," by Katrina and the Waves. It was the joy of their lyrics that kept me singing them for months afterward. I played the songs and danced in our backyard in the sunshine.

It was the 1970s and 1980s, but we watched old movies starring Jerry Lewis and Dean Martin or Doris Day. Again, these were happy, joyful movies. Mum was by nature very sensitive and did not like watching anything that was violent or aggressive.

As I progressed through my primary school years, my sensitivities started to separate me from my peers. I attracted lots of bullies, and I felt overpowered and inadequate.

In the seventh grade, I was getting ready to go to high school the following year. In preparation, we had a transition day, when we visited the local high school. My first encounter there was with the bully from my primary school, who was one year older than me and now attended high school.

He had caused me to shed many tears in primary school. For example, as I walked home from school one day, he had come from behind and pushed me off the footpath on to the main road. Luckily, there had been no cars coming, but I had sprained my wrist as I tried to stop my fall. Now here I was, a year later, and he was handing me a cigarette.

I came home from the transition day upset. I was telling my family what happened when my brother's new girlfriend mentioned that she had attended an all-girl Catholic high school close to our home. Within the week, Mum, Dad, and I were sitting meekly in front of the principal, a very stern nun named Sister Gertrude Mary. After interviewing us, she accepted me. It was the perfect school for me; it was a lot more protected, and it had the faith I craved.

Thank you, universe, for guiding and providing for me.

Empathic Child, Empathic Adult

When I looked back on my childhood, I couldn't understand why it seemed I cried every day. I understand now that I am extremely empathic. When I worked in the corporate world and had regular work reviews, that characteristic always came up: "Paula, you have too much empathy."

I understand now that as a child I took on the energy of those around me, especially in crowds and even at a universal level. It probably would have been good to understand that not all those emotions were mine.

It would happen that, sitting in a restaurant or café, I would tune in to the emotions of those around me. It was if I were being shown their lives. One person would be thinking about a letter received from a friend that morning. Another person would be worried about a sick relative. I always presumed that everyone could do this.

I also had an uncanny connection with people. I once dreamed that my son's teacher was pregnant. When I popped in to see if she was OK, I found out that she *was* pregnant. Months later, I again dreamed about that same teacher holding a little boy with dark hair. As I walked through the school gates, another teacher came up and informed me that the teacher had had a little boy with beautiful thick dark hair just that morning.

As a family, we always talked about our dreams and their meanings. My grandmother would run over and check to see if we were OK if she dreamed about dirty water or teeth falling out. One time I dreamt that my grandmother was on a swing and fell off. I went to see her that morning only to find that she had fallen down her back steps. Thus, as a family, we took these signs very seriously.

My mother's family came from a little country village where there was no doctor in residence. My great-grandmother was the midwife, naturopath, and space clearer. They used local plants to treat ailments, and my grandmother used them with us. Chamomile was the go-to remedy. We boiled it up and used it to wash out our eyes if they were red; we would drink it if we had a stomach ache or if we couldn't sleep. I still use this with my children. From a very young age, my boys would come up and say, "Chamomile, Mummy."

Another plant I remember my grandmother using was *ruta*, which I found out when I was older was the rue plant. This was a bitter plant my Nonna Maria would infuse into alcohol, but we would only consume it for digestive purposes. I'll stick to the chamomile, thank you.

Thank you, universe, for the understanding and the gift of divine timing. You send me the right people at the right time into my world.

Our Soul Families

One thing my journey has taught me is that we do have certain people who turn up in many of our lifetimes. In doing healing on my past lives, I have found many people who I have shared contact with in other lives.

My husband, my children, grandparents, parents, and good friends have all shared lives past and present.

Our soul families are the ones who challenge us; they make us grow, and sometimes we may see it as a struggle. But we must always be grateful for an encounter and see the blessing in the learning.

If members of our soul families challenge us, we must look to expand and grow and change ourselves.

If we encounter resistance in ongoing relationships, we must look for another path.

If there is constant rudeness and disrespect, we must seek to surround ourselves with positivity and light.

We do not need to endure bad behaviour. We can say, "No, I will not put up with this treatment" and turn to the light and live with integrity.

If there are people in our relationships who withhold their love, the blessing is to learn that we do not need to be filled by others but can go within ourselves and be fulfilled.

Sometimes a lesson may be around having boundaries, to say "Enough. Thank you for the learning in this lifetime and in the past, but I have the learning now."

We learn gratitude in these blessings.

Other times we may have loved ones who will share in future lifetimes or we may connect with them now when they are just in pure-energy form. We are linked and connected, and we feel their love and guidance.

An example of a true soul learning for me was meeting my husband.

Rossano and I met on 22 November, 1992. The day had been rainy, and I had gone with some friends to an Italian festival. Rossano had gone to the festival with his friends. As it turned out, my friends and his friends were first cousins. While our friends were catching up, Rossano and I found ourselves talking to each other.

It was interesting, because the moment I saw Rossano there was an instant spark of recognition. That night we stayed on to watch the festival close in a blaze of fireworks above us.

He asked me for my phone number, and as they say, "the rest is history." The first time he rang me, he said, "This is Rossano De Francesca," and the way he said it with such authority and ownership, I just knew he was someone special.

We were together for three years before we had our wedding day. Both of us lived at home with our parents, but we always made time to see each other.

We were faced with challenges to manoeuvre, as is any couple. But each challenge we took on brought us closer, cementing our bond and bringing about mutual respect, admiration, and a very deep love for each other. At times it felt as if it was just the two of us in this very big world, and this continues even today as we take on each beautiful learning.

I understand how much true soulmates can make us grow. They provide us with challenges, so we heal and expand.

My husband has made me question and seek. Rossano is someone who has a very strong moral compass. He lives his life trying to be the best human being he can be. He is someone who will always run to the rescue of another. There have been many times when he has chased a thief who has taken a little old lady's purse and brought the purse back. He has seen someone fall in the street and jumped off his bike to go to the person's aid. He has slid across many the bonnet of a car to rescue an older person who has pressed the accelerator pedal instead of the brake pedal and driven down a shopping centre entrance or crashed into a fence. He has resuscitated people who have collapsed with heart attacks. He offers water and refuge to older people on hot days. He instructs our boys to always do the right thing by people and is teaching them to say no to bad behaviour.

Another example of a member of my soul family is my best friend.

My best friend and I are the third generation of best friends. Her grandmother and mine were best friends, and so were my mum and her mum. To this day we have a solid friendship filled with deep respect.

Our dynamic always fascinates me. We may not speak for two weeks due to busy lifestyles, but when we speak, we find out that during that time the two of us have encountered very similar learnings, although the way the lesson was delivered may have been different.

I also believe that soul family members can come into our lives and then leave once we have done all the work needed, or they may pop into our lives at various stages.

I had a good friend who I met in high school. We always laughed together, and being together made exams and assignment deadlines bearable when we were teenagers. A year after high school, we seemed to just drift away from each other. It just felt like a natural separation. There was no harshness or fighting; it was just a gentle parting. Nearly twenty years later, I was at Kinder Gym with Santino, and I bumped into her. She was there with her daughter, who was only three weeks younger than Santino. It felt as if we just took up where we'd left off, with pure laughter and making light of life.

I have learnt that we pick our parents and our friends for the lessons we need to learn. When I really understood the true meaning of this, it took away all the energy of blame. Things are not being done to me or at me; rather, I know that I picked the lessons.

My sister is another example of soul family. We have had past lives together, and she has been a beautiful example of kindness. She has a compassion for people and, especially, animals. She is generous, kind, and considerate and would always look out for me when I was young.

After Rossano and I met, yes, there were lessons, but it exposed me to another group of friends and family, which offered opportunities to grow.

When there have been immense challenges, I have learnt to send blessings. The people who have demonstrated resistance and their shadow side, I have learnt to look beyond. I would not have been pushed to grow and look for other solutions if I had not received such lessons.

As I have gone through journeys with members of my soul family, I have found that if I listen to my inner guidance then there will be smooth transitions, but whenever I come from reaction and fear, things become tight and feel wrong and harsh.

I am so blessed to have these soul family members. They have shown me their strengths and led me to aspire to be the best version of myself. When they have challenged me, I have grown and looked for other solutions.

Santino

My husband, Rossano, and I had been married for eleven years and had always said that it was up to God to send us children at the right time. We were on the eve of a new year when I received a vision of Rossano and me looking inside a bassinet and seeing the face of a baby boy. I told Rossano when I got this vision that I felt that a baby wanted to join us.

When I first found out I was pregnant, we were so excited we didn't sleep for three nights. I was doing home pregnancy tests but went off to our doctor for a blood test to receive absolute confirmation. On the day the doctor rang me with the results, I was managing the hairdressing salon we had in the northern suburbs of Adelaide. A little bird walked through the shopping centre, past all the other shops, and into our salon. At the exact same time, in our other salon in another part of Adelaide, Rossano had a visit from a little sparrow!

The doctor rang at that moment to tell me that the blood test showed a positive pregnancy result. He also recommended a wonderful obstetrician who had delivered his new grandchild.

Our obstetrician was a wonderful and especially helpful specialist, perfect for a very nervous set of parents. He was authoritarian and reassuring, and he had a collection of handsome bow ties. He was happy to encourage natural birthing, but as his office was attached to a hospital, I took comfort in that, too.

During the pregnancy we took yoga birthing classes, and I was introduced to hypnobirthing, which exposed me to using breath in the body. My birth plan was simple—I wanted it as natural possible but was happy to be guided by our obstetrician for the well-being of my baby and me. I guess this was my first lesson in surrender and handing over control.

Rossano was doing the hair for two weddings on the Saturdays on either side of Santino's due date. With the first wedding we had the back-up of staff in case Rossano was not there, but with the second wedding there was no back-up.

The first wedding came and went, as did Santino's due date. On the Saturday of the second wedding I was still very pregnant. That afternoon Rossano rang me and said, "Wedding all done," and it was at that exact moment that my water broke. The contractions started at fourteen minutes apart and then went down to ten.

At about 3:00 a.m. I rang the hospital, and they said to keep labouring at home. But I was starting to panic a little, so we decided to drive to the hospital, just to check that everything was OK. We got there around 5:30 a.m., but I wasn't even dilated, so the midwife sent me home to walk around and rest.

I tried to have a nap, but the pain was quite intense, so we decided to go for a walk. Around the streets of our suburb we walked, and whenever I had a contraction, I would turn and pretend to peer into a shop window, giving the illusion that everything was fine. It was at one point when I put my arms around Rossano's neck to have him support me through a contraction that people coming out of a church asked us if they needed to ring an ambulance. "It's all OK, thanks; we are fine," we replied. Looking back now, that whole situation still makes me laugh.

By 4:00 p.m., though, I was done. If I was going to labour, I wanted to be in a hospital where I would be monitored; this had gone on long enough. When we got there, I was 5 cm dilated, so that meant I could stay. They still encouraged me to walk around, so we walked around the beautiful grounds of the hospital.

Once the contractions were three minutes apart, they suggested I have a shower, but that really didn't do much. I was exhausted and lay on the bed. The TV show *Australian Idol* was on, and when our obstetrician arrived, he pulled up a chair and watched it with us. All the while I was contracting. I remember leaning over and biting Rossano's arm mid contraction and twisting his arm. As he pulled away, I couldn't understand why he wouldn't let me do it to him. I think I was completely irrational at that stage.

Just before 11:00 p.m. I was finally ready to start pushing. One hour later, still no baby. The obstetrician administered some numbing medication and then tried two goes of the forceps, but again nothing. At that point I really was not in a good place, and Santino's heart rate became erratic. I just remember hearing "Emergency Caesarean" and being given some medicine to drink to prevent vomiting in the operating theatre. As we went up in the lift to the operating theatre, I remember having my top taken off and being dressed in a hospital gown, while Rossano was having papers thrust at him to sign.

The spinal block they gave me was strong, and I became numb from my chin down. Santino was pulled out at 12:38 a.m. on 15 October, 2007, and even though crying, he was blue in colour. After they checked him over, they wrapped him and handed him to me, but I was still so numb all over and terrified of dropping him that I handed him to Rossano to hold.

Before Santino was born, I had made Rossano promise that no matter what happened to me in the delivery of our child he was not to leave the side of our son. As they took Santino down to the nursery, as he was a little distressed, I knew Rossano was by his side the whole time. I was in recovery for a couple of hours, and then I was wheeled into a tiny little room where there was only room for my bed and the bassinet.

There we were at 3:33 a.m., just the three of us, our new family, sitting in this new surreal space. As the sun rose, its rays shone in through the windows of the hospital, symbolising the new—our new life, the welcoming of our new baby. It was one of the most poignant experiences in my life.

Since then I have learnt about the Christ Consciouness light, where a room lights up with such pure, gold light that it resonates at a higher vibration on earth. Such was the light in that little room that morning. That was the light my son brought into this world. Thank you, my darling son.

To my dearest Santino,

Thank you for picking me to be your mummy. You have taught me so much, and I hope I have guided you when you needed it.

I thank you for teaching me what courage really means. You have determination and drive within you such as I have never seen before. You feel the fear but can manoeuvre through it, trusting yourself.

At times it appears that you are holding back and sitting on the sidelines, but I know now that you are taking the opportunity to observe and learn before you immerse yourself fully.

Never forget how divinely spiritual you are. You are always connected to your spirit team and have a beautiful team of guardian and archangels around you.

I give to you the song that I still sing to you:

> Mummy loves Santino, Santino, Santino;
> Mummy loves Santino, yes, I do.
> I love you.
> Mummy loves her baby, her baby, her baby;
> Mummy loves her baby.
> I love you—yes, I do.

I always tell you the story of when I first found out that I was pregnant with you and I told your Pa when he got home from work. You laugh as I tell you that your Pa choked on his pasta and had to cough and cough after I told him the wonderful news.

Your Pa is the one who picked your name; he is a huge *Godfather* fan. Santino "Sonny" was the first-born son, as you are, my darling. I love your name, as it means little saint, just as you are sacred to all of us.

I also love to recall the time that we went and had our passport photos taken. Every time they went to take your photo you would break into that beautiful smile of yours. As you were two, we didn't know how to stop you from smiling or didn't even want to. Eventually we got your smile downgraded into a little smirk, and that was passable for the passport authorities.

That smile has appeared in many a photo. Whenever we were out at a restaurant or café, you would wander over to the other tables, especially if they were singing "Happy Birthday." You would photo-bomb their photos and come back with birthday cake.

Love you, my darling.

Always, your Mummy

Paula De Francesca

Stella

Stella was the first of my babies that I did not get to hold in physical form.

I had no reason to think that there was anything wrong with the pregnancy; everything seemed normal, but I felt sad. My husband, noticing my sadness, suggested, "Let's start sharing the news with everyone."

The obstetrician we'd had for Santino had retired, and I needed to find a new specialist. On contacting her office, I was told that she did not see new patients until at least eight weeks gestation. So there we were on week eight being told that there was no heartbeat. I looked over at Rossano, and I saw grief wash over his face. *I did this to him. I have made him so miserable,* were the thoughts that got stuck in my head in that moment—complete self-blame.

The obstetrician sent me home to see if my body would naturally let go of the pregnancy, as I was just starting to bleed. But after a week of heavy bleeding, I still had to undergo surgery. It was painful, harrowing, and frightening.

When we got home from the obstetrician, I was in shock. My parents were there, excitedly waiting to hear when they would be grandparents again, and instead I had to give them the news. I was numb. My mum, so kind, just wrapped a blanket around me; it felt like I was enveloped in a universal hug.

I could only shake my head; I couldn't speak. I numbly allowed myself to be led to the couch. Santino curled up next to me, and we just sat.

Rossano, in pain and shock, used the pretext of having to fix his sister's TV to leave us. I understand now that he needed to be alone in his grief.

Then we had to tell our family and friends. The one thing I noticed as I told each person was that I got his or her story. There were stories of recent loss but also of losses experienced fifteen, twenty, or even thirty years prior.

As they told me, I could feel their pain. It was as if they were back in the moments of their loss; the emotions were still very raw in them. I decided then that I would not be a woman who was still raw with grief twenty years later. I was going to heal!

The worst advice I received was "Just suck it up and get on with it." *Are you kidding?* I was angry, and I was grieving.

Before Santino was born, my husband and I had started to read books from Wayne Dyer and Louise Hay. We had done a course where we had learnt to inspire staff, but it had begun to transfer across into our everyday lives.

Also, having Santino, we wanted to be the best parents we possibly could be for him—when he was born, we'd experienced such a magnitude of love!

The morning before we were due to see the obstetrician and receive the heartbreaking news, I had bought tickets to a Hay House event in Sydney, where Wayne Dyer was to speak in August of that year. When I finally stood in front of Wayne Dyer at the event, the tears just fell from my eyes, as his presence was so powerful. After the event, he walked straight over to me and I heard him say, "Make the choice. Make the choice to heal," as he held my hand.

My first step in healing was to meet with a practitioner who did EFT Tapping. Rossano had heard about this process from a client, so I booked an appointment. It was a unique experience, and I felt a release. The practitioner tapped the top of my head, eye brows, under eyes, side of eyes, chin, collar bone and under my arm while saying a statement which I repeated which targeted the emotion that was being raised during the session.

During the next six months I was led to see different practitioners. I found those who worked in emotional freedom techniques were of benefit, as that is what I needed to do. I needed to release the emotions.

It was at this time that I started to meditate. Wayne Dyer had a meditation called Getting in the Gap, and every day I would follow this meditation. Some days I would fall asleep, but other days it helped to calm my thoughts and calm me.

I know now that it was the universal Divine Source that was guiding me, to awaken me to the messages of my spirit.

Paula De Francesca

Find another Way

Our neighbours were putting an extension onto their house, and as we shared a laneway, there were constant workmen and trucks coming and going.

The day after I found out that Stella had no heartbeat, I went to take Santino to a doctor's appointment, but a truck which was bringing dirt into the neighbour's property was blocking our exit. I had to wait and wait, which caused us to miss our son's appointment. I was enveloped in grief and hurt. I felt very irrational and at a breaking point.

The next day as I was coming back from shopping, there was a truck delivering a portable toilet to my neighbour's backyard, and I couldn't drive in to my garage. I was done. I parked my car behind the truck, locked it, and went into my house through the front entrance. I heard the doorbell ring but refused to answer it. Only when I heard a voice say, "Police—open the door!" did I come to the gate. With Santino in my arms, I answered. At the gate were a female and a male police officer. "Do you own that car in the laneway?" they asked.

"Yes", I replied, crying. "You don't understand," I explained hysterically. "I can't drive in or drive out of my home anymore." They were calm and professional as they walked Santino and me to my car so that I could move it out of the laneway and allow the truck to leave. I was crying the whole time, tears of grief, frustration, and sadness pouring out of me. I was hurting physically and mentally.

Even as I write this and revisit that space, the hot tears well up in my eyes and run down my cheeks.

From the May until the November of 2010 I was on a mission to let go of the grief. Rossano and I handled our grief differently and very much alone. It was rare that we would come together to talk. I set out on my quest and he on his, and by the December I didn't know how our marriage was going to survive.

It was the week before Christmas, when I was on the phone to my great auntie in Italy. My Zia Carmela was an extremely special person in my life, and even though we lived in different countries, we would travel back and forth to visit.

As we spoke, she said, "Paula, I need you."
I told Rossano what she had said, and he stated, "OK, we need to go."
Looking back, I see that the universe was showing me this lesson.

Your old ways are blocking you; look for a new way.

Paula De Francesca

Italy

We got through Christmas and Boxing Day, but there we were on 27 December standing in front of a travel agent, ready to book our trip to Italy. The universe really must have wanted us to go, as the travel agent was helpful and kind.

One week and five flights later, we arrived late at night in my auntie's city in Italy. The drive through the Italian streets was beautiful, as all the Christmas decorations were still up; they lit up the central square with shiny, angelic blue stars. The next morning it was as if we had experienced an illusion—all the decorations had been taken down.

Our first stop that morning was to see my auntie. There she lay in the hospital, only weighing 35 kilos. Her eyes were closed. She heard our footsteps, turned her head, and opened her eyes. "*I miei tre angeli*—my three angels."

We just held each other, not wanting to let go. I set to work immediately meeting with the doctor and the director of nursing, talking to them about her test results, etc. Within a few days of our arrival she had regained some weight. I could feel that she knew any worries or burdens had now been handed over to us.

We loved spending time with her. She would constantly cuddle Santino, and he would listen to her beautiful Italian words and feel her warmth.

I was constantly inspired by her faith. She told me that every morning in her life she would put her feet down on the ground and would thank God for a brand-new day.

To be in pain, or to be scared or unwell but to have faith was one of the greatest teachings in my life. We need to know that there is help and that there is always something there to catch us, even though we may not be able to see it in that moment.

Being an ex-teacher, my auntie continued to amaze me with her intelligence and thirst for knowledge. She knew many languages and could converse with anyone on any topic.

We stayed with her, enjoying every moment, until one day she went for a nap and slipped peacefully away from us. She was eighty-nine years old.

I organised her funeral, and Rossano said that the way the priest had sung the service was the most beautiful thing he had ever heard.

The burial itself was very confronting. In a busy city like hers, coffins were buried in shelf formation, with many coffins on top of each other and side by side, so one big hole wasn't just for one person's coffin. You could see all the other coffins too. Interestingly, the gravediggers at the graveside were exactly as those portrayed in horror films, all covered in mud, with missing fingers and teeth.

We stayed in Italy for a little while longer, tidying up her affairs. Even though we were in a surreal shock, it felt as though it was the three of us in a whole new world. As I was dealing with business affairs, it enabled Rossano and Santino to have one-on-one time together. Everyone's Italian language expanded, and we immersed ourselves in the culture around us.

Italy is very much a healing place. There are many spots where the vibration is very high. We got to spend a week in Assisi, where we could feel the vibration of the city and its surroundings.

It was two weeks after my auntie's passing, and I was in the office of our lawyer, when all the bells in the town started to chime. Our lawyer looked at me and explained, "Bells chiming brings good news." The next day we were in the town square, watching Santino chase pigeons, when I heard a voice in my ear saying, "You are pregnant with a little boy called Enrico."

After I told Rossano this message, we set about finding the words for "pregnancy test" in Italian. I sent Rossano into a chemist to ask for the test. He came out with the test in one hand and the knowledge that the Italian word for pregnancy is *gravidanza*.

We were worried due to the previous miscarriage, but once again we were shown how supported we were by the universe. A beautiful friend in Italy worked in the city's women and children's hospital. This kind friend was able to secure me an appointment with the top obstetrician there, who was English speaking and specialised in high-risk pregnancies.

When I first met this doctor, he made me smile, as he was straight out of an episode of ER. He had designer green scrubs, a deep tan, gold chains around his neck, and long curly hair. He performed the first ultrasound, but it was still too early to see a heartbeat, and he advised us to come back in two weeks. When we returned, however, he gave Rossano and I the greatest joy when he showed us the heartbeat of our son.

I acknowledge that the universe will lead me back to places and people that feel like home.

Enrico

After Santino's birth, my doctor recommended that I have another Caesarean. I became accepting of this but seemed to be triggered about having to pick my son's birthdate. I always felt that it was such a personal decision that I shouldn't have to control that. I would speak to Enrico as he grew inside of me and say, "This is the birth date picked, but if you want another one you choose it." I was due to have a Caesarean on 21 December, but on 13 December I started to experience early labour, and Enrico was born at 2:38 p.m. on Wednesday, 14 December 2011. The time was very significant to us, as my auntie had passed away at 2:38 p.m. As my Zia had never had any children, I knew that she had met Enrico in spirit and sent him to us, her ultimate gift.

Enrico came into the world with true fear. Unlike Santino, who was born all smiles, Enrico didn't really smile but would cry and cry and cry. Also, during his Caesarean delivery his eye and eyebrow were cut by the scalpel, and he came out quite bruised.

From 7:00 at night until 1:00 a.m. he would cry. The only thing that would calm him was rocking. I would sit in bed with my knees up and put him in between my knees and rock him back and forth. He would look at me and cry.

After weeks of this, I remember, I asked God for guidance. I then came across a website which was based around the book *The Aware Baby*, by Aletha Solter. On consulting the website, I came across instructors who supported parents. I was guided to email one of the instructors. We set up a phone conference, and she explained about really listening to a baby, especially as he raged and cried, so I tried it the next day at naptime. I looked Enrico in the eyes and said, "I love you, and I am listening." He not only cried but also wailed. I repeated it again: "I love you, and I am listening." After one hour of this, he fell into the most peaceful sleep he'd had since he was born.

The instructor explained to me that it was important for parents to be in a state of peace and gave me listening time so I got to express my fears. Once my tightness was gone, then I was able to listen to my baby with an open heart.

From this I was introduced to Hand in Hand Parenting, an organisation set up by Patty

Wipfler. I started to read the articles and do some of the online self-guided classes. I then joined a community group to learn the tools. There were five tools used. We had a beautiful facilitator, plus there was a group of four of us from all over the world who would conference-call regularly.

As I progressed through the year-long training, I was strongly guided to become an instructor of the Hand in Hand tools.

One of the tools was *play listening*, whereby you used play to evoke laughter and release tension in children—but it works for the parents, too! There was *stay listening*, which was what I was doing with Enrico—being present while he offloaded emotions. For some reason, I seemed to be a natural at this, whereas the play listening, the fun stuff, was more of a challenge for me. There was also *special time*, during which you set a timer and let the child pick what he or she would like to do during that time. This fosters wonderful connection between child and parent and allows children to feel empowered.

There was *setting limits*, by which you hold a limit with a child in a loving way, which then leads to offloading of emotions.

I started to really see where my boys would need to offload stored emotions. The crying over a dropped ice cream would be so intense that I knew it wasn't about the ice cream at all but rather being able to offload old hurt and fears.

At the end of the Hand in Hand year-long course, there was an exam to become an instructor. Patty, the founder, rang me herself, and that morning I was able to talk about what had happened just an hour before. Santino had been unwell and had been coughing all night. I wanted to take him to a doctor for a check-up, but the only time I could take him was just before my phone interview. As Patty was in the USA and I was in Australia, we had this time carefully booked.

Rossano was working, so I enlisted my dad to take him to the doctor. Santino had never been to any appointments without me before. I supported Santino as he offloaded his fears of going to the doctor and being unwell and me not being with him. I held the space until he had emptied, and then, when my dad came, they happily went off to the doctor. On their return, my dad said that Santino had done an amazing job of speaking with the doctor and explaining all his symptoms himself. I was able to go through this as an example still very fresh in my mind when I spoke to Patty.

Listening time was another tool used; all would get a set time to offload feelings, with the listener only being there for support. Everyone was free to speak, knowing it was a safe and confidential space and the listener would not put forward any opinion, such as "when it happened to me" or "you should do this." All would be listened to.

I found listening time a challenge at that time. I travelled in anger but couldn't cry for months. Also, I felt tightness that was difficult to unravel.

By this time Enrico was experiencing night terrors. He would go to sleep and then wake up screaming. We would go into his room to find him standing up in his cot, screaming with terror.

He would not focus on us but looked behind us. He would scream and scream and scream, a look of frozen terror on his face.

This is when I would use the *stay listening* tool. I would say, "Mummy and Pa are here, and you are safe." He would yell and yell and then urinate—the ultimate release. I would then wrap him in my arms and hold him as he calmed down.

At this time my husband spoke to a client who was a teacher, and she apprised him of a lady who did kinesiology and specialised in healing of children. I booked Enrico in immediately.

She was able to determine that he wasn't coping with the EMF (electromotive force) around him. This made a lot of sense, as we were staying in a five-storey apartment building at the time, and the energy was very erratic and electric.

Not long after we met her, she told us that she had finished training in Holographic Kinetics, an advanced Aboriginal healing modality, and we did a session for Enrico. The process was to call through Enrico's spirit and remove trauma.

Both my husband and I started to have sessions. We went to another practitioner who also practised this modality, and we began to see amazing changes in Enrico. It really supported us by alleviating stresses around parenting.

One morning I was due to have a Holographic Kinetic session, when Enrico woke up with scratches on his back that had not been there before. I went off to the appointment, mentioning these scratches to the practitioner immediately. I became a surrogate for Enrico's spirit, and we went back to a past life where he had been in a war. It had been very cold, and he had suffered frostbite along his spine. During the session this trauma was healed, and when I got home, the scratches had disappeared just as quickly as they had appeared.

I realise now that our spirits know when we are ready to heal and what we need to let go of. Sometimes before a healing session there will be obstacles, blocks to getting to the session on time. This can be our egos, our fears, not wanting to let go of something. I often saw this in the early days of my own personal healing sessions. I would be on the way to my healer, and there would be road works, stop signs, and burst water pipes. When I did my session, there would always be something very deep that I wanted to let go of but didn't know at a conscience level. I had fear around what would replace the pain if I didn't have it anymore.

Now it is very different. I surrender to my learning. I am open to explore, no matter how deep it may be, and I know that once it is gone it will be replaced with joy and love and lightness.

As a toddler, Enrico was one who needed to be number one. As we started going to Kinder Gym and Cirkidz, I would turn to look for him, and he would always be the first in line. This confirms the reason he chose to come into this world two weeks early.

Even now, he has a way of connecting with people at a really deep level—and they let him go first. He was born with the belief that he is deserving to be out there and to be heard. He has been an amazing teacher to me, as I was the one who would inch myself back and back and back until I disappeared.

Enrico sometimes gets frustrated at school, as he has so much information downloading, which he then wants to share. But he must wait for his turn and listen to others. He gets upset if he is not allowed to fully empty and tell the story, and he does not like being interrupted mid thought.

I look in awe at my boys, the way they manoeuvre their relationships and their school lives. They really are born at a time where we are seeing the school systems change and adapt to the needs of the individual child. Every child is different and learns in his or her own way. It is beautiful to see the teachers showing new ways of learning and inspiring.

The children of today are coming in with a voice and a purpose in an era of more acceptance than ever. They do not have to fit into constraints and pretend to be something they are not. They are listened to and can articulate the need for changes.

My boys have been my biggest change makers. I see how fearless they are. I see the school they go to embrace acceptance.

When a child stands up and makes a speech, instead of being laughed at or embarrassed, he is encouraged and celebrated.

If a child falls and hurts himself, a friend will help him, a second will comfort him, and a third will run and get help from an adult.

The children are aware of a friend who may be having a rough day, and they will comfort and reassure this friend without being prompted.

Instead of children criticising others to make themselves feel better, there is the thought that *If you can do it, I can do it too.*

Thoughts of not being enough are diminished, to be replaced with *What can we do for the betterment of humanity, for others?*

The children shop at the local market, cut up vegetables, and make soup to feed those who are hungry.

They knit scarves for the homeless, and as they knit, they discuss the situations that cause the homelessness that people are experiencing and what they can do to prevent it.

There is evidence of social consciousness at such a young age.

We can be fulfilled when we help others, but we do not have to diminish our own lights to do this.

We can shine, and the more we shine, the more we encourage others.

Paula De Francesca

To my darling Enrico,

Thank you for the lessons you brought into this world. From the day you made yourself known in that piazza, when I heard your voice for the first time whispering into my ear, to every day since, I thank you for being you.

I thank you for your bright inquisitive eyes and your beautiful questions stalling every night our brief departure from one another.

I love the wonderful way you engage with people. Even as a baby, you would ask people, "What's your number?" and everyone would be happy to tell you their age with beautiful warmth and sincerity.

Never forget how wonderful you are.

Thank you for showing our family what it is like to be a leader, to put yourself first but with empathy to others and fairness.

You showed me that it is OK to have a voice, my darling, and I am grateful for this.

For you and your brother I became an advocate of your needs and well-being.

I admire you for your deep thoughts and desire to share these thoughts with the world. You are heard, my darling—you are heard.

Always yours, with so much love in my heart.

Your Mummy

Attachment

My spirit has led me to experience situations that I would not have known possible. My physical body, however, quivered at every new opportunity and courageous act.

I was asked to speak in a video on the transition process of children starting school and how important it is to allow children more time in their potential new environment. To be in front of a green screen and be interviewed would have left me horrified years ago, but now it has instead left me wanting more and loving the experience.

As part of his fear, Enrico had a lot of trouble letting go of me. Through the Parenting by Connection tools, we worked on separation plus used the healing modalities.

At night he would always want to be wrapped in my dressing gown, and to this day he loves being enveloped like a big hug within its softness.

When Enrico was three, we introduced him to a preschool, but he never settled or enjoyed it, so we chose not to send him. When he was four, we tried a kindergarten, but he would leap out of the teacher's arms and lunge for the door if I left. He would sit at the door until they rang me to come and get him. He stopped sleeping, and if he did sleep, he would wake screaming. Fortunately, at this time both Rossano and I were working from home, so we decided that Enrico did not need to attend any preschool or kindergarten.

Once again, the universe supported us. The teacher that Enrico was due to have for his first year at school was the same one Santino had had when he'd first started, so Enrico was familiar with her. Also, she welcomed us to visit her classroom six months prior to Enrico starting school. Three times a week Enrico and I would go into her classroom, and as the months progressed, this wonderful teacher would set me little tasks which would require me to walk a little away from Enrico. If I was doing a job for the teacher in the library, he would still be able to see me. I would always leave my bag, phone, or car key with him, so he knew I wasn't very far from him and had not left.

All through this time we were doing lots of healing, including healing on me. He was my baby, and a lot of the separation angst was coming from me. I couldn't let go.

Enrico was a baby who would hang onto me. He was always in a baby sling, and I loved how he would feel against me, while he would love the comfort of my heartbeat. For months I would sleep sitting upright with him in my arms, to the point where I developed a bald spot from rubbing my head on the bed head! Once again, after losing Stella, there was a lot of fear coming from me.

The universe shows me connection.

The universe shows me support.

The universe shows me healing.

Breastfeeding

With Santino was born, we had him in our room. Then one day I asked Rossano to put him down for his nap, and Rossano came back empty-handed. I asked him where Santino was, and he replied, "You told me to put him down." He'd put him in his room in his cot, and he was happy to be there. I'd breastfed him for two years, but the day I stopped he developed an attachment to his teddy bear which he had not had before. Weaning him of breastfeeding was a difficult process, and I did not think he was ready, but I received so much flak from people around me whose own insecurities washed over me continuously.

This experience was a learning experience for me. It taught me that the times when I wavered in my beliefs I would encounter people to challenge me, either to completely break me down or to make me stronger.

I also learned that other people got triggered too, and I needed to recognise this. It was OK not to be around people who were being affected by my choices.

This was extremely evident with Santino and breastfeeding. I loved nursing him; it was our time of connection, with his beautiful blue eyes looking up at me and mine down at him. It felt as if we were truly one. Santino would refer to breastfeeding as *mono*—his nickname for Mummy's milk. I would use a muslin cloth to cover him, not for the benefit of others but to allow him his quiet time. He would pull the cloth over himself, especially if the surroundings were too noisy.

Santino was twenty-one months when we went to Italy. We all contracted swine flu, and as the weather was so hot and I was breastfeeding and vomiting, I became dehydrated. When we arrived at a little village to visit some relatives, I fainted, and a kind relative took me to the local doctor. When I explained that I had been unwell and that I was breastfeeding, even the village doctor said, "What? Are you going to breastfeed until he goes to the military?" With that comment he saluted and snapped his heels together.

It was surprising, too, how many people, especially men, saw breastfeeding as a very sexual thing. I would receive lewd comments about my son and how he would grow up. Or people would say, "You are so creepy. You get so much pleasure; that's why you don't want to give it up."

Also, people who were unable to breastfeed their children were the ones who were very quick to say, "You need to stop; you are not doing him any favours." I never realised that breastfeeding my child would be such a controversial topic.

I know now that I had a big learning around asking for what I wanted and holding my true beliefs strong.

I needed to honour my true feelings instead of allowing the pressure of others to stop me.

If I am confident and truly believe, then I know that I will not receive resistance.

It was important that I learn to really believe in myself.

With Enrico, I was adamant that he would choose when to stop breastfeeding. I blocked everyone's comments out and only tuned in to my son. Enrico stopped breastfeeding at three years and three months. It was at this point that he started to use breastfeeding to get my attention. If I was talking to someone, he would climb up onto my lap and try to breastfeed.

I also recognised that he would want to breastfeed when he wanted to stuff down feelings and stop crying, and at these times I would use the Stay Listening tool. I welcomed him to empty his feelings, holding him and listening as he emptied any emotions that were bubbling under the surface.

Rossano and I spoke to Enrico and explained how he could now choose a cup and try different milks to drink. Thus his transition was a beautiful experience.

The more of my healing work I do, the more I find that babies need to be conversed with. If they need to go to the doctor, they need to be told, and if they are going to be examined, they want to be asked, regardless of their age. Even babies of two weeks of age want to be consulted, especially if they are going to have something invasive done, such as a doctor's examination.

I know that in my own healing and that of others, birth trauma comes up a lot, and therefore healing of our births is very important. So is the understanding that we pick our parents and experiences. Thus we grow and expand and learn, knowing that we are supported through the process, no matter how uncomfortable or empty we may feel.

So many children's spirits that I have worked with, as well as my own, have said, "Please treat me as an equal."

"Talk to me. Tell me what is going on."

"Ask me if it's OK to be examined by a doctor or nurse. Don't presume that I don't understand, because I do."

The spirit of a foetus that has yet to be born can already talk about the preparation of its birth and its purpose for this new life on earth. Some already know their guardian angels and want to clear past-life trauma even before they are born.

I am so honoured to give voices to these babies through their spirits.

A New Modality, and the Spiritual Floodgates Open

While Enrico was little, as a family we were having healing sessions, and we could see the benefits. At this time, the founder of Holographic Kinetics was coming to Adelaide to undertake a practitioner-training session, which I attended. It turned out to be a truly life-changing and amazing experience.

The training was phenomenal! There was so much healing done, plus I got to step up and become a practitioner. I started to practise this healing modality, undertaking sessions for whoever would volunteer. Each client offered an amazing learning experience.

After completing my Hand in Hand training, I was put in contact with a listening partner who was based interstate. We would take turns off loading our feelings and discussing the tools used to support our children. One day she asked if she could have a session with me. Now, with Holographic Kinetics you can do remote healing, but you need a surrogate, so I asked my husband to surrogate.

First off, though, it is important to clear the surrogate of their emotional baggage so that they can do the role. Unfortunately (or fortunately), by the time I had gone through all my husband's healing he was exhausted and unable to surrogate.

I sat in meditation and asked, "How am I going to do this?"

It was then I heard a voice in my head say, *Just call through her spirit.* I was told to draw the outline of the physical body, and I was then guided to the points on the diagram where trauma was being stored and instructed to clear the trauma.

At first, clients would contact me with their priority issues, and I would go away and do the session with their spirits and then contact them with the outcome. This took a very long time, even though the results were amazing. I was then guided to do healing sessions in person or over the phone but to have the person with me at the time, so I could explain exactly what was going on and even get feedback as we went through the process.

Paula De Francesca

The healing sessions constantly evolved, with spirit showing that true healing happens when we are ready. We then let go of things that no longer serve us and replace them with more lightness and joy.

As I sit with clients, their spirits work through me to heal their traumas. The beautiful thing with spirit is that there is always a validation of the healing.

For example, one day when I was doing a session with a client his spirit kept clearing lessons around lack of personal boundaries in the past and respecting his time and space. He was denying his passions and was getting caught up in the drama of friends and family. His spirit kept saying, "People come into your space and dump their drama on you and leave." Over and over in the session it kept coming up, so we worked on clearing all the issues in this lifetime as well as past lives, when this pattern was set up.

Just as we finished the session, a council truck drove up and dumped a whole load of manure at the front of his house. This was a true validation of asking him, "How much more of this do you want to take on?" After the session, the client was able to hold stronger boundaries around his needs. He took steps to distance himself from people who were drawing on his energy and worked to attract new, peaceful friends into his life.

Thank you, spirit, for leading me through the healing and allowing me to let go of what I no longer need.

Thank you, spirit, for the lightness, joy, and hope you bring.

Spiritual Knowledge and Awakening

I have always loved gaining knowledge, but I felt that as soon as I hit forty my learning tripled. This coincided with my awakening of spiritual development. I was led to learn, read, and absorb information. I undertook learning in different modalities, did research on chakras, adopted a daily yoga practice, and expanded my knowledge in any ways that I was guided.

I was guided to research the clair senses, to determine which one of my senses was strongest when I tuned in to spirit. On reflection, I'd always had intuition, trusting my gut instinct, but as I started doing my spiritual courses, the inner voice on the right side of my head was getting louder. I would start to see a movie or visions play out through my third eye.

At first the voice was faint, and I went out and purchased a set of earmuffs so that I could tune out all external noises and only concentrate on spirit. It wasn't too long, though, before the voice and feelings became very strong, and I could get guidance even in a crowd.

While I was learning about the different spiritual modalities, I found a YouTube episode of a spiritual teacher undertaking a meditation. As I went through the meditation, I felt my uncle step forward. He was such a lovely man who had passed away a few years earlier. As he came through, I could feel his energy immediately, and I could hear him in my inner ear, talking to me. It was such a beautiful feeling having him around, and it felt reassuring.

Shortly after that, more loved ones who had passed over started to come through. The more spiritual healing work I did, the more spirit started to knock on the door. It started to disturb my sleep—they were around all the time! I was guided to work on my boundaries and to set up closing and opening times. Then I was guided to say, "When I am in session, then I will listen."

Then it went to, "Only if your family is seeing me as a client can you step forward during their session."

As for my family members and good family friends who have passed over, such as my auntie and grandmother, they pretty much appear whenever they want, through signs. Every time I think of them, they step forward—or is it that every time they are around, I think of them? It feels like a full circle. There are always signs, such as songs, smells, words, or prayers.

On occasions when a person who has passed over needs to get my attention, the indicators on my car get turned on and off. It seems that they are telling me to change direction. I will flick the indicator up, and it will be returned to normal position. As this is happening, my car clock or odometer will show the numbers 444, indicating that angels and spirit are sending through a message.

Sometimes I will hear a random song in my head over and over and over, and it does not leave until I relay a message to the relevant person.

Our loved ones want us to know that they hear us, not just at their gravesides but when we talk to them, or acknowledge them, or look at photos of them. Anytime they come into our minds they are there hearing us and offering us comfort if it is needed.

As I connect with more and more people who have passed over, they talk about the learnings and growth they are experiencing on the other side. Sometimes they show me that they have connected with their friends who have also passed over.

A friend's mother who was a devout Catholic came through, showing me that she had connected with her friends who had also passed over; they were continuing to pray together. I was shown this lady and her friends sitting around in a circle, with bibles on their laps, praying.

If the person was a big lover of food and different cuisines, I will see them walking through a beautiful big kitchen, lifting the lids and smelling the beautiful food cooking.

A loved one who has passed may show up holding a baby or a pet who has also passed, indicating that the baby or animal is not alone in spirit.

Occasionally I have witnessed spirits helping loved ones who has passed to clear some of their past patterns and beliefs. They have confirmed that they are always learning and sometimes will apologise for their actions on earth, as during their life reviews in spirit they have had the opportunity to see how their actions affected their family and friends. They acknowledge this new understanding and learning.

I have also been shown that when people on earth are suffering from dementia, the times when they seem vague or unresponsive are really occasions where they are going back to earlier times and reliving memories so that they can heal from those times. When they do come back to present time, they sometimes seem agitated, as they have just relived a past memory and brought the feeling of that time back with them. These people are doing a lot of their healing even before they pass over into spirit form. They tell me that, as they are just sitting around, they may as well do some work and get a jump-start on their healing process!

I have had situations in which people who have passed over via drug overdose or substance abuse still must do a lot of work in their healing journey, but as they are no longer attached to a body or earth, the information is clearer and messages more powerful. Their energy will feel a lot lower, and sometimes they do feel that there is still some resistance in their energy. I am always shown that they have their spirit teams around them if they need support in the healing process. But there is an understanding that they must heal in their own time.

Thank you, spirit, for the ability to always heal and grow

Nonna Maria

As my grandmother grew older and became a widow, she remained living in her house, but as she did not want to sleep in the house alone, she would come over to our house around 5:30 p.m. every day. After she passed away, Mum and Dad's doorbell would ring every day at 5:30 p.m. for a full year.

My grandmother was ninety-one when she passed over into spirit form. My mum and dad tried to keep her in her own home and then in their house for as long as they could, but it got to the point that Mum couldn't lift her anymore. My parents made the decision to put her in a nursing home close by, for what turned out to be the last six months of her life. I would visit often, and as I was pregnant with Santino, I was able to show her the ultrasound photos of our baby.

When I was six months pregnant, there was one day when I just felt off; I cried and cried all day and all night. I had no idea what was going on. The next morning, I got a phone call to say that my grandmother had passed away. I felt that I'd needed to have that cry and let go of grief so that during the process of her death and funeral I was able to step up and organise things and be present.

The day after her funeral I went for my check-up with the obstetrician. I was exhausted, and he told us that our son was positioned at an awkward angle, so it was hard to see if he was growing. With this statement and with all the emotions from Nonna's passing and funeral, I was done. I started to cry and cry. I was exhausted, emotionally drained, and worried about our baby. That night I woke up at 3:00 a.m. I put on the TV and started to watch an episode of *Crossing Over with John Edward*. He was doing a reading on someone in the audience and brought through the person's grandmother, who said, "Thank you for organising everything for my funeral. Thank you for writing the eulogy. Thank you for supporting the family." I felt the goose bumps come up all over my body. I knew that this message was for me. It was from my grandmother.

I had written her eulogy, which my father had proudly delivered. Even that eulogy was divinely inspired, detailing her life, and telling how proud we had been of her.

I felt immense relief and healing.

Once again, the universe had sent me a healing tool and a messenger when I needed it most.

Thank you, God. You knew when I needed you most.

Mediumship Energy: We Are All Connected

One night when Enrico was small, I was nursing him, and to stay awake I had my iPad on the stool next to me. Enrico stretched and kicked the iPad, which caused the iPad to switch to an old talk show. The episode was about a family who had a member missing, presumed dead. When I went back to bed, I was awakened by the family member who had disappeared, and he told me what had happened. I didn't know what to do, as all of this was still very new to me. The incident wasn't even in my country, so I just wrote everything down and sat on it for a day. The next night he came through again, with more information, and then the following night again. It was after day three that I sent an email to the family detailing the information and explaining exactly who I was. I received confirmation later that they had been able to resolve this missing-person case.

I was in meditation one day when the spirit of a person came through. I heard the voice say, "Please help!" I was guided to connect with this spirit and was told that he was in hospital having a transplant. The surgery was life-threatening, as the condition was very rare. I was told to go back to this person's past life, where I found that he had been a volcano in a past life, and this volcano had erupted, killing many people. This person had the spirits of the people killed still attached; they all needed to be freed. I was guided to free the spirits and allow them to transition over, which cleared the karma of the volcano. Weeks later, I was watching a news report that featured a patient who had been released from hospital after a transplant from a rare condition. I knew that this was the person. Years later I saw a follow-up segment about this person, and he was healthy and living a beautiful, fulfilled life.

There was another instance, in my home state, when a prominent football coach passed away. The day before he passed over, my uncle came through, saying, "Paula, there is going to be a family argument, and a man with a name starting with P, is going to pass away. My son is going to be very upset." My cousin was a huge AFL football fan.

The next day we woke up to hear on the news that this coach had indeed passed away. I was due to do some spiritual work that day, but the energy across Adelaide was so low that I couldn't tune in to any high vibrations. It showed me that we really are affected by outside energy, not just our own. It felt as if the whole city was grieving and in shock. There was a blanket of heavy energy all over the city.

Highly tuned to my spirit and that of others now, I can stand next to someone and want to vomit if his or her energy is not right. Even hearing a song on the radio can make me feel sick. I will then research the artist and find that he was convicted of rape or had taken someone's life.

Also, if people are under the influence of drugs, including prescription drugs or alcohol, I can feel that. It makes me feel sick or off balance, and I will need to shift my energy away.

I get very affected by big crowds and find myself exhausted, especially after visiting big shopping malls, cinemas, or concerts.

For a long weekend once, my husband organised for us to go away. Usually I am tour manager for our family, but I was in pure surrender mode, so he made all the arrangements. The place we went, however, was painful for me. The whole time we were there I felt as if I had three books weighing down on my crown and third eye. Harsh energy was visibly apparent in this town, with evidence of vandalism to properties and people yelling and swearing. As we walked down the street, a drinking glass was thrown off the balcony of a hotel and smashed at our feet. As we crossed the border and came home, I felt the books lift and all the pressure come off. The town had extensive history, and the energy was quite low in vibration; it was physically painful for me. My legs swelled up, and the children and I had nightmares the entire time we were there. My husband said that he had never seen anyone wanting to leave somewhere so fast—by 2:00 a.m. I was already packed and ready to drive home!

Thank you, spirit, for healing and protecting us.

Paula De Francesca

The Archangels

As I started doing more guided meditations, I began to connect with and get to know the various angels. I would feel their energy surround me, and then they would always validate their presence with signs.

As I drive around a lot, I always have a podcast on from a spiritual healer or inspirational person. I am discerning of who I allow into my space and do not listen to any negative, hateful speeches or watch television shows that contain violence or horror.

Archangel Nathaniel

One day I was learning about Archangel Nathaniel when I turned onto an unfamiliar road. When I looked at the street sign, it said Nathaniel Way.

Archangel Michael

Archangel Michael has such a strong presence, and he always makes me feel so safe. I was in a bookshop one day, and a pack of oracle cards flew off the shelf and landed at my feet. This pack of oracle cards didn't just fall—it travelled a metre in distance and connected with my legs. It was a pack of Archangel Michael oracle cards.

My son Santino was having his confirmation and had chosen St Raphael as his patron saint. As we learnt more about St Raphael's life, we found that he was one of the saints who became an angel. Santino said he loved Raphael's green energy, which surrounded him on a regular basis. In the bookshop, Santino picked a little statue of Raphael to mark the occasion. It came in a box, and both the shop assistant and Rossano checked the box. When we got home and took the statue out of the box, it was Archangel Michael, complete with his shield.

Archangel Michael always comes through with such strength and protection, and I am so honoured to be able to connect with him.

I always visualise a royal-blue velvet cloak enveloping me from head to toe when I need protection, or I ask Michael and his band of angels to surround my home.

I always see the royal blue and deep purple around Michael, but it is his strength and security that I feel.

I had an incident with a new client one day, when the client became aggressive and lunged at me. At that point Archangel Michael caught his fist and said, "No, you are not getting through." It was the lower energy that needed to leave the person's body. The next time I saw the client, he had a beautiful statue of Archangel Michael in his home and he was telling me of the miracles in his life that had occurred since he started talking to Archangel Michael.

Archangel Raphael

One day I was driving and talking to Archangel Raphael; I needed his healing as I was feeling very flat and sore. I saw a bright-green car pull out in front of me. When I looked in my rear-vision mirror, the exact same colour and make of car was behind me, and then a cyclist, in the same colour green outfit with matching helmet, whizzed by me on his bike.

Whenever Archangel Raphael is around and sending healing, I will always see beautiful green rays of light coming through. Raphael is such a beautiful and powerful healing angel.

The Father, the Son, and the Holy Spirit

Whenever I need the reassurance of Spirit, I will see the number 33, 333, 3333, or 3.33. It is always reassurance of the Holy Trinity—the Father, Son, and Holy Spirit—which is the comforting energy coming through, reassuring me, loving me, and guiding me. I can see the word *Jesus* or hear someone mention his name, and I will look over and see 3:33 on the oven clock, the time on my phone, or a page number as I open a book. Over and over this appears, as validation that I am not alone.

Especially if I do get a fearful moment or there is a very earthly feeling of worry or being overwhelmed, I will always see the number in that moment. It is just such a visual reminder, saying, "Paula, snap out of it. You are safe, we are here, keep going."

I had always asked for protection from Jesus, Mother Mary, and God and the Saints, as I was brought up saying my prayers every night and going to church, but it has been such a lovely blessing to learn to connect with the angels, too.

Whenever I feel frightened, I always recite the Our Father, the Hail Mary, and the Glory Be over and over. I always benefit from the beautiful healing and calmness.

One night, just after losing Stella, I couldn't sleep. I lay in my bed, in mental pain, and I thought, *How am I going to get through another day?* It was at that point that Santino woke up. I went into his room and started to rock him in my arms. As I sat in the chair, I felt a comforting hand on my right shoulder and heard, "Paula, you are not alone." I could feel that it was my grandmother, and I could feel God. I knew I was not alone.

When I was little, my dad's mother was very sick, but she had such faith in Saint Anthony of Padua that she prayed to him to be healed. She prayed and believed, and she was healed of the medical condition that had plagued her.

I remember one Christmas Eve not too long ago, when I was standing in the city's cathedral. The congregation was singing "Silent Night" and the setting sun streamed in through the stained-glass windows. This beautiful light brought in the Christ light of Christmas, and I felt angel bumps travel through my whole body as I felt this healing and inspiration.

Mother Mary

After my first miscarriage, I would go to St Raphael's Catholic Church and pray. I would kneel in front of a statue of Mother Mary and talk to her and ask her for guidance and strength.

I was in the practice of pulling an oracle card out daily and receiving the guidance from spirit that accompanied the card. On Mother's Day I said to Mother Mary, "I really should pick a card relating to you, Mother Mary, as I need to honour you and thank you for always helping me." As I scanned my hand over the various decks, I felt for the one that was hot. I put my hand over a deck honouring Mother Mary, but I kept hearing her say to me, "It's not about me." I was drawn to pick another box of oracle cards, not the Mother Mary ones, but I still felt that I needed to pull one out from the Mother Mary deck to show her how grateful I was to have her in my life.

I pulled the deck out, and as I shuffled the cards, I was guided to pull a certain one out. On it was the word *God* and a picture symbolising God's presence. I heard Mother Mary say very clearly to me, "It is always God working through me and through all of us."

When I look down on my laptop as I am writing this story, I see that the word count is 33333—once again she passes all glory and honour to spirit. She doesn't need accolades or to be put on a pedestal. She is so humble and honourable, but her strength is so powerful.

Even right in this minute, as I recall these wonderful messages from Mother Mary, I am guided to pull another card, and the one that comes out is Anna, the mother of Mary. Mother Mary is honouring her own mother and showing me what a wonderful woman she was. Mother Mary is an amazing teacher, one of honour and humility such as I honestly have never witnessed before.

Another number I see a lot is 555, 55, or 5.55. This is a reminder of Archangel Metatron around me all the time. The energy is always around having a purpose, about putting one foot in front of the other. It's a call to action. There isn't just a feeling of security but one of confidence, which says, "You've got this; we've got you."

When I started doing my spiritual work, Archangel Metatron would always pop up with signs. The more I connected with the energy, the more the validation and signs would appear around me. I would be listening to a meditation on Archangel Metatron, open a random drawer, and would see a picture of this archangel.

I can think of Archangel Metatron while driving and see four orange cars, all the exact same model and make, following each other. It is Archangel Metatron coming through on golden rays, guiding humanity.

There are so many beautiful angels who come through with different messages, and it is such a beautiful gift to be visually reminded all the time.

So many times they have helped and protected me, and I always feel that someone "has my back."

The more I connect with the angels, the more I am shown that they are here to support me and that I must be open to asking for help.

I understand now that connecting with the angels and asking for help does not take them away from someone else who needs their help—in fact, they have shown me that this multiplies the healing for everyone.

One morning as I was driving home after school drop-off, I was listening to a podcast about numbers and their angelic meaning. Every number that was spoken about showed up in the number plate of the cars to one side of me, in front of me, to the other side, and in back of me—even in the phone numbers on the sides of vans at the exact moment that they were mentioned.

I laughed as I saw the number plates of 123, 456, 789 surround me and heard Archangel Metatron say, "Life really is easy as 1-2-3."

"OK, OK, I hear you," I said.

The next morning, feeling a big cheeky, I said to Archangel Metatron, "I bet you can't go backwards."

"Here, I heard," was the response, and as I looked around there was a car to my right with 987, in front with 654, to my left with 321—and let's throw in three rows of cars all ending in 000!

I can do anything as long as I trust and surrender.

Guardian Angels

Connecting with my guardian angels came through meditation. I would protect my space by envisaging a gold bubble around my whole body, and then I would relax my body and ask my guardian angels to come through and introduce themselves.

I visualised myself sitting on a park bench and asking my guardian angels to come sit beside me and share my space.

The first angels to come through and introduce themselves were Paul and Renee. It's interesting, because when I was a child and right through to my late teens, I'd always wanted to be called Renee.

I was guided to say, "Thank you for being around me. You know what I need today. Please help me to help others. I am surrounded by your love at all times. Show me evidence of kindness and love in every step."

They are always happy to help, but I needed to learn that I was deserving of their help; it was OK to ask.

One day I walked into my bedroom with my hands full. I asked my angels, "Could you turn on the light, please?" The light turned on. "Thank you, guys," I always say. It is so important to be grateful too.

Another day I was cleaning around my bed when the side of the bed came out of the frame. The heavy wood fell, but before it landed on my foot, it was caught and put back into the frame. Once again, I had some wonderful help from my beautiful angels.

Another time I was carrying a stack of chairs down some stairs, and I said, "Some help would be appreciated here, please." Before I had finished asking, one side of the stack became very light, and I could feel Archangel Michael helping me carry the chairs. As we reached the bottom, Archangel Uriel popped up too, saying, "You are very welcome."

A wonderful teaching regarding surrender that I heard one day was comparing it to going into a restaurant. We decide what we want from the menu and then we give the waiter our order. We can then imagine how lovely that beautiful food is going to taste. We do not have to go into the kitchen, source the food, cook it, and then serve it to our table. We just put the order in and know that we will get something amazing in return. We truly surrender into the belief that everything will be amazing.

The other beautiful learning that I have heard from a messenger was from publisher Abraham Hicks. If we try to control our lives from our own viewpoint, it can keep us quite small. But if we leave it to the universe, then it can be far more expansive than we ever imagined, because it is from the universal viewpoint.

Abraham Hicks also teaches us to look for evidence of beautiful things appearing in our lives. When we set this intent every morning before even putting our feet on the floor, it is already out in the universe. The second part of this exercise is exciting too, as I then get to look for the evidence of this intent.

For example, I might ask, "Please show me evidence of kindness today." Then, as the day progresses, I will see a kind act or a kind smile, things showing up to match the intent.

I completely trust that I am always helped because I listen to the guidance every day.

I set my intent for the day with purpose, and for this I am grateful.

Letter to My Spirit Team and Angels

To my most honoured spirit team and angels,

I thank you for your support. I understand now that you are happy to help all of us and that your love and assistance will never run out. The more we act in true faith and are guided by you, the more we can multiple your healing with others.

I will continue to listen and to be guided. I accept your help so that I may help others.

Thank you for giving me this amazing gift of being able to hear, see, feel, and know that you are always around.

For this I am eternally grateful.

Paula

Miracles and Magic

Miracle

One day I woke up to a phone call from my husband that on his way to work he had seen a lot of police cars blocking off the road next to our street. He then sent me a link stating that a bush fire was burning on the hill next to our house. He told me to activate our bush-fire plan and to evacuate. Before I reacted in fear, I walked calmly outside. I couldn't see or smell smoke, and I looked up to the sky and said, "God, do you want me to evacuate?"

In that moment I heard very clearly, "We've got this; you are safe." At that instant, it started to rain. I felt completely safe and cocooned, not at all fearful.

This experience was a validating experience, as over the previous weeks I had been encountering a lot of people who were travelling in a state of fear. They were always talking about their worries and concerns. They were consumed by the media and were watching it 24/7. This playing out in front of me made me retreat more and more into the energy of the angels and spirits. I felt safe. Every day I worked with a purpose, and I just kept going forward with motivation.

I am so grateful for the feeling of comfort and ease.

Magic

There was another time, when we had promised our boys that we would go see fireworks. It was New Year's Eve, and we had booked a hotel overlooking the ocean. My beautiful little boys were so excited to see the fireworks explode in all the beautiful colours. There would be a 9:30 p.m. showing, which they called "the family fireworks"; the organisers knew that a lot of little ones could not stay up to midnight.

But as I stood there in the dark and quiet of our hotel room while my boys slept, I looked out the window and watched the second lot of fireworks being set off at midnight. I felt completely immersed in their magic. As we were on the eleventh floor of the hotel, I was directly in line with the exploding colours. I had been reading Radleigh Valentine's book *How to Be Your Own Genie* at the time. He wrote about witnessing the magic in your life, and here, completely aligned to the blazing colours of red, blue, green, purple, and gold, were these magnificent examples of light reflecting onto the calm ocean floor. I could feel the excitement coming up from the people below. I was in a state of awe and gratitude for being able to witness all this true magic in physical form.

I love to see the magic and miracles in human form.

Rebelling against the Guidance

It seems that sometimes as humans we rebel against the guidance from our Divine. In me there was a deep-seated belief that I was not deserving of help. I would challenge the guidance of any help from spirit or human.

One day we were at the shops, and my son wanted a ball filled with slime. I heard my guidance say, "Do not let him have it—no way!" But I gave in to pressure from my boys; besides, my son used his birthday money to buy it. Two days later I heard a cry-out from upstairs, and as I rounded the corner, I saw that there was slime everywhere. The slime was on the carpet, walls, and TV. I was angry with myself for not listening to the guidance. It was a very interesting lesson to wake me up.

I had another incident in which the very human part of me wanted to test the guidance again. I had some paintings in my garage which I wanted to hang in the house. As I picked up one picture, I heard very clearly, "This picture is not to go inside of your home." I picked up the picture anyway, took it inside the house, and went to hang it on a picture hook. It was then that the hook on the wall and the hanger on the back of the picture both broke. "This picture is not to go inside of your house. It is old energy and does not belong in this house." I promptly turned around and started back out the house with the picture, nearly tripping over it in my haste to get it out.

I do that with food, too. Knowing that certain foods are not good for my body, I will have occasions when I am upset and will reach for chocolate and put it in my mouth. The chocolate will taste like metal. "You do not need this," I will hear.

I know when I act out like this that it is a red flag to show me that something is not right. It means that I need to centre and realign myself once again.

Help me to let go of any rebellion against your guidance.
I let go of the fear and ego that drives me to this and only
surrender to your guidance.

Connie

In May 2016 I was well on the way on my spiritual journey. I was dealing with spirit every day and in complete connection with the personality of spirits and their messages.

It was during this time that Connie stepped forward to introduce herself to me. I got to know who she was in her past lives and knew what she needed to look at. I understood that she needed to heal herself and that there were lots of lessons about her needing to feel safe.

I always had a belief that I would have a daughter, and I thought that this little girl coming through this time was going to stay with us.

We found a lovely obstetrician, and because of the past miscarriage, he started to monitor me from six weeks' gestation. He would do a scan every week, watching the growth and waiting for the heartbeat. By week seven there was still no heartbeat, but he gave it an extra week just in case our dates were wrong. Unfortunately, on week eight there was no growth or heartbeat. As soon as he confirmed this, I was scheduled for a dilatation and curettage that night.

With Connie, I felt her spirit go from within me in a second. It was Mother's Day, and one minute I could feel connection to her spirit, and then in the next second she was out of my body. "I won't be safe here on earth" was what I heard her say to me. The next day was when it was confirmed that there was no heartbeat.

Those weeks were difficult, as once again Rossano and I went to our separate corners, grieving alone, trying to take away each other's pain but not knowing how.

**My dear Connie, may you always find safety and peace
in your journey. Thank you for connecting with me. I am
grateful for your presence.**

Lucy

In August 2016 I felt a little girl spirit around me. She introduced herself to me as Lucy. She kept showing herself in a wheelchair and blind, but she was so beautiful. She kept saying, "I do not want to have another lifetime like this."

I took a pregnancy test which showed up as positive, but within two days I felt her spirit leave me. This was a natural miscarriage, so initially it felt a lot quicker and less intrusive; however, two weeks later I started to bleed and needed to go for ultrasounds and tests. This showed me that I hadn't dealt with the grief; I needed to really heal from this lesson.

Once again, I was led to books to help me heal and practitioners to help me clear trauma. I connected with Lucy's spirit and found that she needed to let go of old beliefs that were keeping her blind. She had experienced trauma, and as the body did not want to see the trauma, it had locked in the blindness. I was shown that she was being healed in spirit form and she was working through her lessons and gaining understanding.

Thank you, my beautiful little girl. May your healing allow you to learn and grow, and may you always be protected, my love.

Our Home Energy

As we entered 2017, my husband kept showing me pictures of houses and suggesting that it might be time to move. At that same time, I was being guided to different learnings, and one of them was Denise Linn's clutter-clearing course. In one of her lessons was a teaching on how to connect to the spirit of a home.

I commenced the meditation, and the spirit of our home stepped forward. The spirit said her name was Lucybell; she thanked me for taking such good care of the home and acknowledged that we had worked together in adapting the house to the changes in our life. I was guided to look up the name on YouTube, where I found a song called "Angel" by a band called Lucybell. The lyrics were listed, and there was a beautiful picture of an angel, exactly as she had portrayed herself to me. The words were magnificent and poignant. It was interesting to me that even though we had lived in that home for seventeen years, it wasn't until then that I'd met the spirit of this home. It seemed that I needed to meet the spirit at that point so she could let go of us.

Looking for houses is a unique experience when you are empathic. I would walk into a house at an open inspection and be hit with the emotions of the argument that the family had had just prior to leaving their house and preparing it for the opening.

I remember looking at one house and, as I walked towards the pool area, feeling violently ill. I could sense that there had been an incident around a near drowning in that pool.

Another time the universe would make me notice smells in the house which were unpleasant, and that was another way of showing me that this was not the house for us.

I could feel if the previous family had been happy or if the house was being sold due to a divorce or separation. I have found out since that there are what is called the three Ds in the real estate industry, three events which can affect the sale of a house. These are divorce, debt, or death. Well, as for me, I can feel the energy of all three.

One day I was looking at some houses on my own in a suburb I had never visited. I started to feel immensely sad and started to cry. Tears and sobs just started to come out of me. Through the veil of tears, I rounded the corner and found a gravesite and a crematorium.

This experience once again validated for me that the signs I got from the universe were spot on.

Also, as part of the process of selling our home and moving, I was conscience of clearing our energy from our home and making it inviting for prospective buyers.

We needed to hire a storage unit during the moving process. The storage unit was opposite a gravesite, and one day as I was in the car park, I could feel that there were bones underneath the soil.

Thank you, darling Lucybell, spirit of our home, for keeping us warm and safe for all those years.

New Home: Our House of Healing

Just as finding a new home was a learning experience, so was the selling process. I used my guidance and my deep gut feeling in selecting an agent. I visualised a gold shining beacon showing potential buyers our home, but ultimately there were some big lessons for us.

Houses around us would be selling twenty-four hours after being listed on the market or not even being advertised, but ours took months. That was because the new house that we were to buy was not ready to be listed yet. It was not listed on the market until five months later. Also during that time, we were given chances to go out and explore all over South Australia, to show us where we needed to live.

The day we saw our new house, the four of us stood on the grass opposite and the sunshine enveloped us. Everything was gold and magical.

I connected with the energy of this new house, and it said, "You are welcome here. It will be very much a healing space for your family."

The first day we moved into our new home, I bent down and saw on the kitchen floor a blue love heart with the word *courage* written on it. Courage has been the operative word for this journey.

After we had been living in our new home for a few months, I realised that everything I had wished for in a home was included in this property. The colours, location, and surroundings were all just what I had wanted. It had many birds that surrounded us and welcomed us daily. There were trees and hills that constantly sent out healing to the universe and to us.

Thank you for showing me what wishes look like in material form.

Courage is defined thus in the *Cambridge Dictionary*:

1. the ability to control your fear in a dangerous or difficult situation;
2. to be brave and confident enough to do what you believe in;

Lori

It was 2018, and in the November prior we had just moved into our new home. Rossano had been contemplating and then preparing to have an operation for an umbilical hernia. He was enveloped in fear. On the night of the surgery, I had a vision of his surgeon being assisted and spiritually guided. I felt a sense of peace wash over me. Rossano's recovery was amazing; even the surgeon was shocked by how quick it was.

With all the fear left behind, there was space for another pregnancy to enter our family. As soon as I found out I was pregnant, I was in shock. I knew it would end in another miscarriage.

I started to tune in to the baby's energy, trying to meet him. He did not step forward immediately. Instead, I met one of his guardian angels, called Vanessa, who was extremely prominent in overseeing him.

This baby spirit was constantly flanked by three guardian angels.

"We've got this," I heard.

Paul and Renee, my guardian angels, Archangel Raphael, and Jesus all surrounded me, saying, "*We've got you.*" I had to just surrender to them. They were helping me, and I was to surrender to the Divine and be healed.

From the moment I got this guidance, the pregnancy process was very different. I didn't push timing; I didn't get anxious over taking twenty pregnancy tests a day and waiting for the results. I didn't force doctors to see me and do scans. Instead, this time I was guided to take a step back and allow myself to be directed. I waited until I was guided to make a doctor's appointed. I didn't keep forcing the Divine to show me this baby. I allowed the whole process to unfold in the exact timing of how the universe needed it.

During the days of my pregnancy, I felt surrender and support at a whole deeper level. There wasn't just one person saying hello and showing me kindness daily; I was in a shop and three shop assistants were helping me.

I saw the same obstetrician again as I had with Connie's miscarriage, and he was as caring as ever. On the second visit there was a heartbeat, but it was very slow. He said it was a lot slower than he would have liked, but he scheduled a follow-up appointment for the next week.

Over the two days following, I could almost feel the heartbeat slowing down, and I knew the minute it stopped beating. There was much grief in knowing that I was carrying a baby, albeit so tiny, and that he had passed over inside of me.

At our next visit our obstetrician confirmed the lack of heartbeat, and he scheduled me for a dilatation and curettage that same night.

I left his office to prepare for the operation, which was not due until after five o'clock that evening. Enrico had football training after school, so Rossano and I headed over to watch him before he dropped me off at the hospital. I was standing on the sidelines when a mum handed me a baby from another mother. I had never seen this mother or this baby boy before, and there he was, thrust into my arms. I held this smiling, happy baby for the next hour, all the while wondering why I had been left holding him when in two hours I was going to have to say goodbye to my baby. Even now it feels as if it came from just a place of acceptance, that ability to physically hold a baby before giving him back.

This whole pregnancy was led by the mantra of "surrender and support."

On the evening of my dilatation and curettage, I was the last person in the day surgery waiting room. In my paper slippers, open-back surgical gown, and hat, I laughed at the irony of this room. It reminded me more of an airport business-class lounge than a place where people would go to wait for their operations.

The nurses and anaesthetist were lovely people, very kind and friendly. But when I awakened in the recovery room, the nurse came over to apologise for my being awakened to the sound of a baby crying. My anaesthetist had been rushed away to assist in a Caesarean birth, and the nurse wanted to ensure that I was OK. She was very sorry that after what I had gone through I would awaken to a new life entering the world. She was visibly upset, so I took her hand and told her that it was OK; it wasn't her fault. I went on to tell her about my beautiful two sons at home.

This lovely nurse and another had finished their shift just as I was ready to go home, so they walked me out to the car park where Rossano and my boys were waiting to take me home.

It was at that point I was able to meet our son. He came forward but still flanked by his guardian angels. My baby said, "I like that you are drawn to the name Lorenzo, but I want to be called Lori." He told me that he had been severely burnt in his past life but was rushing back into a physical body, as he wanted to continue living his life. He told me that he still needed to heal, and he needed to do his healing in spirit form, where he could get the learnings and guidance he needed at a deeper level.

I asked him why he'd picked us as parents, and he said, "I knew you would understand."

I also knew there was learning in this for me. I needed to look at my reproductive area and deep-seated beliefs.

To have had three dilatation and curettages, a natural miscarriage, and two Caesareans meant lots of scarring, so again I needed to address the learnings around this. Why was there so much trauma surrounding my reproductive area?

To my dear reproductive system,

I want to firstly apologise to you for the guilt that you have been raised in. I feel that I have put so much pressure on you for being dirty or not good enough.

Instead, I want to thank you—thank you for giving me my two beautiful boys. You supported them as they grew and birthed them.

Thank you for giving me the opportunities of meeting beautiful people and for the gifts of healing.

I want to acknowledge all parts of you and want you to know that you are wanted. You contribute to my fertility, and I love that.

I am sorry for any tears or pain you have stored and had to endure. I welcome the lightness and unconditional love for you.

Paula

Healing

As my pregnancy with Lori ended, I was shocked that I was to have surgery again. I realised that my body was shouting at me. I needed to do more work around beliefs concerning intimacy and sexuality. I had been brought up in a Catholic family with very strong beliefs that intimacy was bad and enveloped in guilt.

The big thought that came up when I was pregnant with Lori was this: "If something goes wrong, it will be my fault." I would be an older mother, so it would be all my fault if anything happened. Guilt and self-blame all came up, ready for me to let go of them.

It's interesting that as I wrote this book, I was guided to do some serious healing work around opening the pelvis and reproductive area. As I moved trauma through the body, I cried for hours, letting go of the hurt as my body shook. Through yoga, breath work, and meditation, I was finally connecting and being appreciative of my body. I no longer criticised it, and I banished all thoughts of me not being good enough.

All through my twenties I'd suffered with a very tight jaw; some days I hadn't even been able to open my mouth. It wasn't until much later that I realised that the jaw is where we hold our emotions.

Also, just recently I was told that in yoga opening the hips and pelvis relates to tightness in the jaw. I commenced doing lots of hip circles and hip-opening exercises.

During the time when my jaw was so tight, I came across a massage therapist who specialised in myofascial technique. She was able to release the fascia of the muscles to provide relief.

It's interesting to me, as I reflect on my healing journey and the practitioners who came into my life, that most of them were strong women who were wonderful examples to me. They were healers and powerful, and it is interesting that these women, one by one, appeared in my life at different stages, all bringing through their different healing modalities.

After the loss of Lori, I suffered a bladder infection, the first one I'd ever had in my life. As I experienced the pain, I realised it was my bladder trying to get my attention; the fever was the anger erupting inside of me. My bladder was letting go of old beliefs, but I was so scared of what the new would look like that I didn't want to let it go. I physically felt the stripping of the bladder of old beliefs, and I gave permission to be shown what the new would look like. As the symptoms of headache, fever, blood in my urine, and pain in my pelvis and lower back appeared, I just kept going within and asking for what was needed.

I kept asking my body, "How can I support you?"

I kept feeling fear and vulnerability.

"I am afraid! What do I look like if I am not shielded in pain?" my body yelled at me.

Once again, I surrendered to the guidance and allowed help to enter my life. I allowed myself to be healed.

So many people have experienced grief and pregnancy losses. After being told time and time again that I was too empathic, I acknowledged that this was a blessing. I could use this to help others—I didn't need to shut down from it.

To my dear body,

Thank you for supporting me in my life. You rolled with the punches and you supported me through all my changes. You expanded and grew. You healed and shared. You loved me and showed me unconditional love, and you continue to support me every minute of every day.

I am sorry for all the times I ignored you during moments of self-loathing. I made you wait for water, food, sleep, and even love and acknowledgement.

Now I know how important it is to nourish you, to listen to you, to love you, and to accept you, no matter what society says you are "supposed" to look like.

I am accepting of every part of you and every change you make every day.

I give you rest, warmth, nourishment, and love, and I promise I will do this every single day until I transition out of this body back into spirit.

Paula

Paula De Francesca

Surrender

On my journey, I have been shown time and time again that when we come here on earth and as we start on our life paths, we come in fully supported. Yes, we will have lessons to help us evolve and grow, but not once will we be left on our own. We have been given our spirit team to help us and physical messengers to support us.

It is important to let go of all *old* beliefs:

The universe is out to get me.
God wants me to suffer.
I have dues to pay.
I have to suffer before my luck will turn.

Instead, replace them with these:

The voice of spirit is always worded with encouragement, guidance, direction, and positivity. It is never harsh or negative.

The feeling of spirit is high in vibration and love.

Spirit appears in nature, joy, symbols of rainbows, roses, birds, and pure love.

When I am in the space of surrender, the universe sends me guidance which I can hear and feel. I receive help by way of physical messengers.

Meditating, going within, and being in a quiet space will help me to hear the guidance.

I understand that I am being given information all the time. If I do not understand, I can ask to be shown another way or request more information.

It is important that I create a dialogue with the angels; they guide me and respond to my questions. They are my best friends, and they are here to help us all.

I was away in a hotel and couldn't connect to the hotel's Wi-Fi, so was using the data from my phone. As I fell asleep, I wondered whether I was getting close to my data limit. In the morning when I awoke, there was a message on my phone that said, "You have 100 per cent data, plus you have a new month of data free."

At that same hotel, I left my brush behind on the bathroom bench. When I got home, I saw that my husband had selected a new brush for me—without even knowing that I had left my other brush behind.

Another time my boys had been unwell, and I had spent all day in the kitchen, organising food and cups of herbal tea and running around. Before I went to bed, I knew there were more things left on the kitchen bench, but I was too tired to do anymore tidying up for the day. When I walked into the kitchen the next morning, it had all been cleaned up by my husband.

There was a time where we had some challenges with my son, and we didn't know what the next step was going to be. Instead of going into fear or worry, I just sat quietly and asked for help from God. Within five minutes I felt a ringing in my right ear, which signalled that I was getting a download of information at a frequency too fast for me to hear. Within twenty-four hours I received physical messengers supporting me with some solutions, plus I had a massive surge in creativity—I was given the downloads of forty-four guidance cards with all their meanings dictated through me. As I received all the messages, I then reflected before bed about what I would need to do for the graphics. Previously I would have taken photos and then gotten the guidance when I held the photo. At 5:00 the next morning, I was woken up, completely refreshed, and told to design graphics. In fact, as I sat at my computer, I felt that spirit was working through me but so fast that I just needed to step aside and let it drive completely.

Before the Easter of 2019 I kept hearing message after message that this Easter light would bring in a whole new meaning. As I woke to see Notre Dame burning, I kept hearing spirit say, "You do not need a building to see me; I am working through everyone and everything on this planet." In that holy week I was also told by spirit that as a human race we needed to fulfil our life purposes and live our lives with meaning, kindness, and connection.

I could hear Mother Earth—Gaia—saying that as humans we are not waking up quickly enough. Within one day of receiving this message, I started to hear that more people were taking on spiritual work full time. I was encouraged to guide others, to help them be the best version of themselves and to live their lives in kindness.

I was told repeatedly that every child being born now is coming in with a purpose. We can no longer squander away our lives but must live them fulfilled and with connection and love for others.

After Easter it felt that we had indeed shifted our vibration, and I was shown the example of going up a lift. We might start in the basement, pressing the button, but then we travel up to level 4, then 9, and then maybe land at the penthouse. With each level, the spiritual vibration is lighter and filled with even more love. I did notice that my body seemed to be stuck in between floors; instead of doing exercise on my yoga mat, I would just sit there and meditate. This lasted for a few weeks, but then my body felt as if it had transitioned. I was able to connect with a huge surge of energy in body, and spirit was even stronger and louder than before.

Thank you, universe, for sending messengers to me.

Divine Timing

As I reflect on the lessons that I have been shown, I realise that there has been a huge lesson around timing. Just as I have been shown the timing around selling and finding a new home, the timing within a pregnancy, and even the timing for little things such as finding a car park, I get examples of perfect timing.

As I went through my late teens, twenties, and even early thirties, I studied and worked, but nothing felt like a perfect fit. I felt like Cinderella without the perfect-fitting shoe. But the more I was led to my healing work and helping others as a messenger, the more it felt like coming home. It was beyond perfection.

In my role as a messenger of spirit, I finally felt that this was my calling. I understand that finding this calling at that exact time was how it was meant to be. I was meant to have experiences and life lessons to be able to help others and to understand deep gratitude.

Everything is in perfect timing.

It is so important to surrender to the timing and not push and push against something that gives us much resistance. It may be that it is not meant for us at that time, and we may need to let it go for a bit.

I understand that even if we are running late for something it is meant to keep us safe.

One day I was driving around listening to a podcast and looking for a car park, but I needed to circle the block a few times. I kept hearing, "You need to hear the rest of this talk." When the speaker was finished, I found a car park immediately. I had needed to hear the message.

There are times when I try to catch up with someone and we just keep missing each other, over and over; we just can't seem to get together. I have learnt now that it is better just to let it go and then wait until I am being shown when to reach out again.

I had an incident when my boys were a bit unwell, but I was unsure whether to send them to school or not. I kept hearing the guidance, "Do not send them to school today." Listening to my guidance, I bundled them up on the couch all nice and warm. An hour later I received a news report that a car had crashed through the fence and play equipment of the park near that school at the exact time that I would have been pulling up there.

Years ago, my husband and I were on a long-awaited honeymoon, and we had arrived in Singapore. Unfortunately, Rossano was unwell and became bedridden. He was so disappointed, as he had purposely picked this location so he could attend a technology expo that was being held. As he was sick the entire time, we did not get to leave the hotel until the day of our departure. In the car going to the airport, we passed a burnt-out shell of a bus. When we asked what had happened, the driver said that a tourist bus transporting passengers from the technology expo to our hotel had been in an accident and been destroyed by fire. We knew that we had been scheduled to be on that bus but had been protected. There was such an inner knowing which Rossano and I felt immediately.

Thank you for teaching me not to push and push against a brick wall but rather to look for the door that is already open.

Advocate

Finding My Voice and Being an Advocate for My Children and for Me—Finally

It was easier to have a voice for another and be an advocate, especially for my children, than it was to stand up for myself.

One year when Enrico started his new school term, he was coming home coughing every day. I took him to our doctor, and she said that he was having a reaction to mould. We had just had our house checked and knew that it wasn't in our home. Besides, at night and on weekends he wasn't coughing; it was only at school and after school. Also, every morning when I walked into the classroom I noticed that it smelled like a mop that had been left in stagnant water. It would make me gag. I am so highly sensitive to smells, but I didn't know whether others were experiencing this as well.

I had to muster so much courage to go and speak to the principal. I kept getting told, "Don't rock the boat. You are going to be known as the troublemaker," but I understand that that was just my inner fears being vocalised by those around me. The school staff were amazing. They undertook tests and fixed the problem immediately, Enrico's coughing stopped as soon as it was fixed. I had to believe in myself to have a voice. The universe seemed to be easing me into this process instead of dropping me feet-first into it. It was lovely, too, as I also received validation by way of the teachers and other parents thanking me for speaking up.

On reflection, I remembered that when I was a child I'd had a dummy. I find now through my healing sessions that our spirit will always acknowledge whether we had a dummy to quieten us. Mum and Dad told me it had been very difficult for me to let go of my dummy, and I had been quite old when they finally convinced me to get rid of it. I know now that I was using the dummy to quieten myself, again relating to not having a voice and not trusting myself or the guidance.

This teaching about having a voice came through very strongly as I commenced writing this book. For three months I felt as if I were in a tunnel, wading through mud. I knew there was an opening, but I couldn't see it. I had received lessons in which I saw that I needed to stand up and state what I really wanted in my life, be it in relationships, the way I wanted to be treated, or what I was guided to say. Physically my body was carrying a lot of fear. My jaw locked up, and I developed blood blisters in my mouth. My solar plexus, the position of power, felt as if I were carrying a big rock, and then it felt as if my solar plexus was being torn in half. I knew I needed to keep going in faith, even though I couldn't see the light at the end of the tunnel. I kept talking to God and my angels.

"Please help, stay close, help me through this," I prayed. I kept stepping closer and closer. The steps felt tiny, but I knew in my heart I was getting close to the breakthrough, the big lesson; I knew I would be shown the growth.

When I was guided to sleep, I slept. I journaled and meditated, and I cried—deep, wrenching sobs such as I had never experienced before. It felt as if I were purging, emptying out the pain of experiences not only in this lifetime but also past ones, lives in which I had been a washerwoman, a servant to others, or of lower class in a society of many classes.

I needed to learn to value myself. That included my time, my body, and my guidance.

I was again doing Louise Hay's course, *Mirror Work: 21 Days to Heal Your Life*. I had done it two times before, but this time there was a section on appreciating the body, and something just clicked. I acknowledged that my beautiful body had carried me through so much in this lifetime, from the changes in childhood through to adulthood. I came out of a year during which I finally forgave and acknowledged my reproductive area, my pelvis, and here I was thanking my body for carrying me through it all. I started to want to give back to it. I understood now what people meant when they said they treated their bodies like temples, giving them good food and love. I was grateful. I no longer wanted to criticise my body or berate it; instead, I wanted to celebrate all that it had done.

For me this journey was about how I become so intertwined in the lives of everyone around me that I needed to become whole again and to acknowledge my own needs.

Thank you, spirit. When I look in the mirror now, I see you smiling back at me and through me.

Celebrating Me

Through my life I have kept myself small, not celebrating successes but downplaying them.

My grandmother died on my eighth birthday, and my grandfather died on my father's birthday, when I was only five months old. This validated my belief in minimising celebrations.

Also, if we were going to any family outing or party, we were never told about it until just before we left, so I never learnt anticipation or excitement.

In grade seven, when I was graduating primary school, the teachers gave out awards to certain students. I was told that I was going to get one, so I did get a little excited—only to be told the next day that the teachers had changed their minds and I would not be getting anything. It added to the belief of not celebrating and of not deserving. In the end I did receive a book and a certificate, but a lot of the celebratory energy had been diminished.

When in my twenties, I worked in the corporate world, and by my early thirties I was part of a dynamic sales team. When iconic companies were renewed or acquired, the sales managers would blow a horn and celebrate, but when I signed customers, I would downplay my success.

I pretty much went through life under the radar, thinking it was important not to draw too much attention to myself.

I so wanted to be invisible that if we were at a function, like a dinner dance, and they had raffle tickets, I would be thinking, *Please, I don't want to win*—because I didn't want to be the centre of attention. I didn't want to have to go on stage!

I remember that as a child I often hid behind my parents. When I was ten, I had to go to the city library and ask for a book that I had put on hold. The librarian told me very sternly that I had not picked it up on time and they no longer had it. The mirrors of insecurity reflected the way I doubted myself instead of being confident and believing.

Even as an adult, if I went to a party the host would come and start introductions. He or she would introduce everyone, but when it got to me, would completely skip me, looking straight through me as if I were not there.

When I was a kid, if they wanted volunteers to come on stage during a concert, I would make myself invisible and never be picked. The thought of being picked terrified me beyond belief. Now I can understand why this is such a big lesson for me to learn in this lifetime.

At shops I wouldn't be served, and I would not be called upon in any training session I attended. I studied Italian when in my teens, and at the end of the course we all had to present a report done in Italian. Everyone got up and presented, but I was not selected, so I never got to give my report, even though I had worked so hard on it. Once again, the thought of standing up and representing myself terrified me, and I allowed myself to be ignored and invisible.

In July 2018 I attended a writer's workshop in Melbourne. I felt extremely intimidated being there; I felt that I didn't belong. I wasn't a writer—what was I doing there?

During the session, Reid Tracy, the CEO of Hay House, stood right next to me, handing out books. I shrunk down in my seat, making myself invisible and small.

When I came back into the session after lunch, I had done such an amazing job of making myself invisible that when I returned to my seat someone else was sitting in it. The person who I had sat next to all morning and exchanged conversation with said to me, "No one was sitting here this morning." I moved to another seat with the inner knowledge that I needed to sit next to someone else, and that I needed to get the lesson.

The funny thing was that when I was picked up from the airport on that trip to Melbourne and driven to my hotel, I had seen numerous number plates on cars around me that said *God* and *joy*.

When I got to my hotel room and looked out of the window, I saw a billboard opposite rotating different signs and words. As I watched it rotate, it suddenly stopped on the word *joyful*, and there it stayed until the following day, when it started to rotate again.

With my auntie in Italy, I had to be an advocate, and not in English either. I was in a different country with a different language, but I just did what I had to because I was doing it for my auntie, who I loved so much and who needed me. I had an inner strength, and I was guided in every step.

Through this whole process I have had to ask for what I want. I am deserving of good things, and it is OK to say, "This is what I need right now."

Even as I write this page, acknowledging this huge lesson, my neighbour's house alarm is going off. The siren is loud, as if saying, "I am here! Can you hear me?"

But it really has taken writing this book to make me stop and celebrate. I celebrate my children's achievements and try to be there for all their assemblies, if they are getting awards, and on the sidelines when they are playing sport. We do try to teach our sons that it is important to celebrate not just the wins but also their achievements and those of the people on their teams.

It is important to celebrate life and to do it while still alive, not at a funeral in a eulogy or just for that one day being remembered.

I am finally learning to celebrate my accomplishments, such as writing this book, I celebrated when I had written fifteen thousand words and then thirty thousand. I was not going to hold off celebrations. Instead, I was going to acknowledge and be grateful.

Thank you, universe, for all your validation.

Thank you, universe, I can stand up and ask for what I need now.

Thank you, universe, for holding me in the space of celebration.

I'm Deserving

For me, the biggest learning has been the blessing of getting to know my spirit team. First it was spirit, our energy, the Divine, God. Instead of looking outside of myself, I learned to know that spirit is within me. The voice that I hear is predominately on the right side of my brain and in my right ear. The vision I see is like a movie running through my third eye. The feelings I feel through my whole body are goose bumps. I feel in my solar plexus a deep need or a sick feeling if something or someone next to me shouldn't be in my space.

I know that Jesus, Mother Mary, and a guardian angel or archangel are around. I know that one of the saints is stepping forward with support or advice. I see the signs from the archangels: their rays of light and their words spelt out in front of me.

Messages are reflected in oracle cards I use when I ask questions or need validation.

The messages are heard and then validated through a physical sign to ensure all doubt is removed.

This journey of this lifetime has shown me what it is to be connected to God and know that the divine is all around. I know that the angels are enabling me to connect with spirit at such a deep level of surrender that it has completely changed my life and continues to guide me every day.

It is to see miracle after miracle, to be open to possibilities, and to silence ego and doubt. It is to have courage to question and investigate deeper.

As I write this book, I have realised one thing: we are all here to fulfil our own life's purpose. I was caught up in thinking there was not enough room for me or that others had already done what I was supposed to do. Yes, there are people doing similar things—there are mums raising children, there are spiritual healers being guided to help people, there are authors—but no one is like me. No one has had the exact experience and situations that I have had. Yes, we may receive the same learning or need to go through the same things but not in the exact situation.

So, the big learning is that I just happened to be in a room of like-minded people. Just like people coming together to watch a sports game, they're all coming together and doing what they love.

I might receive a sign or guidance, and I acknowledge that it is to help me on my life path, step by step, going forward. It reminds me that I am never alone.

I could be walking along with someone else who won't notice what I saw, but they may notice something else that is meant for them.

When I was at the Hay House Writer's Workshop in Melbourne, there were over three hundred people in that room. I was intimidated, thinking, *How could I write a book when all these other people are doing it too?* But you know what? Everyone had a different story to tell, or maybe each was there for a different reason.

I know that I would not be so divinely driven and guided to share my story if it was not meant to help someone. There is someone who needs to receive comfort or a learning from these words. They come not from me or from ego but from spirit sending them through me.

Everyone has a story filled with learnings and teachings to share with others.

Paula De Francesca

Darkness

On this journey I have also been shown that sometimes there is the darkness of shadows and evil.

I have learned that sometimes we depress our vibration to lower levels, and it attracts negative energy, which attaches itself to us. We are no longer listening to our spirit, for there is so much negative gunk weighing us down that we are no longer speaking from spirit but are only hearing fear. With a lower vibration, there is an attraction to alcohol and prescription or non-prescription drugs, which keep the vibration low and dull the spirit.

Also, if we keep holding on to pain instead of freeing it from the body, it continues to block the flow of our energy. We get layers of fear upon fear, and it fills us up completely, just as the feelings of love and joy heighten our vibration.

I had an incident when I was driving down the street and saw a girl picking at her skin. She was completely out of her body, and there was negative energy running her. It was awful; I felt sick, as she was just a shell of her body filled with darkness eating at her body. I was reassured, though, that she was not in pain, because her spirit had left the body, so she did not realise the pain of this. As I drove by this person, the lights changed, and I stopped for the red light. My spirit said, "Paula, look away. Do not look at that again." Of course, my streak of rebellion led me to look again. Just as I turned my head, a big bus pulled up alongside of me, blocking my view, and I heard my spirit reiterate, "No, Paula, you do not need to look at this again!"

As I walk down streets, I can often see the negative energy slithering around in front of certain hotels.

Another time I was on the phone talking to someone who was having struggles with her family member. I'd had encounters before with this family member and knew that her energy travelled at a very low vibration. I pulled to a stop behind a car at a traffic light and noticed that the car in front of me had an evil symbol on the back of it. As I looked to my left, I saw that I was in front of the person's house that my friend had been telling me about. It just showed me again that this person was weighed down with negative energy and it was best not to be around her.

Sometimes if someone does get blanketed in negative energy, he or she can remove it by detoxing their diet, refraining from alcohol and drugs, and working towards changing thought patterns, connecting with nature, and clearing the negative energy.

I always pray and trust that when the time is right the negative energy from a person will be lifted. Unfortunately, it is during that time that horrible acts can be committed. People who are intoxicated and out of body drive cars and cause accidents; they commit murders and vicious acts to others. That is why I am such a firm believer in keeping our vibration as high as possible all the time. I don't allow any negative energy to invade my space. I protect my energy, especially if I go into a crowd or into a place that doesn't feel light.

Hospitals are a hard place for me to be, as I get hit with all the pain and suffering people are experiencing as soon as I walk in the door.

Some places also have more history attached to them, and that I can also feel.

I remember someone telling me that he had done a tour of the old Adelaide Gaol and had to leave because he'd become violently ill. I was guided to explain that he was feeling the residual energy of the place. Also, if there are large tour groups going through places, you can feel their energy too.

Sometimes I would take my sons to school by a different way, and every time I did this, Enrico would become agitated and cry at the exact same location. He would say to me, "Mummy, I don't know why I'm crying." When I took note of the location where this was occurring, I realised that we were passing the site of Adelaide's old hospital. There was so much sickness and memories of death trapped into the soil.

I have been told by spirit that this location and that of some others in Adelaide would benefit from deep indigenous healing of the land.

I have noticed with our dog that she would be asleep on the seat in the car, and then she would sit upright and start to bark and bark. Usually she has a cute little bark, but this was the bark of a little dog trying to make herself bigger out of fear. Each time she did this at the same point, and I realised that across the road was Adelaide's prison. She could feel the energy coming from behind the barbwire.

When I have a massage, I need to envision the gold bubble around myself; otherwise I can feel the energy of the massage therapist. One time my friend and I went to have massages as a birthday treat for one another. As the therapist started to massage me, I could feel that she had had a fight with her sister that morning and was still running it over in her mind. I could feel the harsh words she had exchanged; I could feel waves of anger coming off her. It even felt as if the whole room had taken on the anger.

Even as I walk past members of the public, I feel that I can scan them and just know their stories—whether they are in relationships, if they are happy, or where they are holding their vibration. It is a strong knowing, like a movie of their lives.

When I was little, I could never swallow meat. I would also become sick after eating different foods, and as I got older the food sensitivities started to become more prominent. As my intuition expanded, I started to feel the energy of the food I was cooking and preparing. I would pick up a piece of fruit and feel that it had been sprayed. I would touch a product and know that it had been manufactured by people who had experienced anguish or by a factory that had very harsh energy.

By the time I was twenty I was vegetarian; my body always feels so much better when I keep a vegan lifestyle. I will walk past a butcher shop and feel the anguish of the animals or the sadness from chickens over being boxed and transported.

I acknowledge the blessings of who we are.

Honouring Those We Allow into Our Space

Sometimes we are challenged by people, and they help us to expand and grow. But after the lesson they will naturally just fade away from our lives, or sometimes we will decide to walk away when we know the lesson is finished. I believe, however, that if we walk too soon, we may have the lesson repeated, but delivered by other people who come into our lives.

That happened to me just before Enrico was born. There was someone who I considered a friend, but every time I had to spend any time with her, I would walk away feeling drained and suffering a headache. Every time I came across her, she seemed harsher and harsher and was exceedingly critical of others. I knew that I needed to distance myself and sever all ties. One day we all had to have a photo taken together, and when I saw the photo, this person was quite shadowed and all her teeth and gums were black, even though everyone else in the photo was fine.

This person was also consuming a lot of alcohol, so I knew she was no longer connected to her body and couldn't hear the guidance of her spirit no matter how hard it was trying to get through. She became a danger, driving intoxicated and being volatile, and I completely distanced myself from her.

Months later I saw her at a function, and as she looked at me my blood turned ice-cold. I had heard this expression but had never experienced it. I felt myself go ice cold from head to toe, and I started to experience breast pain. I was breastfeeding Enrico at the time, but within twenty minutes of seeing this person I was enveloped in a fever. It manifested into mastitis, and I became bedridden.

I have since learnt that I need to believe in my spirit. I now know that it is very strong and that I cannot give my power away to anyone or anything.

I have learnt to breathe and start my day by saying, "I hold my light of you working through

Paula De Francesca

me, spirit. Please show me the true personality of everyone I meet today, and let everyone be transparent." I am then shown evidence of people's personality traits immediately.

I believe that my spirit is always strong and powerful; it is not affected by anyone else's energy.

Shielding and Protection

I am grateful for the training I did through Holographic Kinetics, as it was very good in setting up a procedure to not let lower energy attach to one's body. Also, I am a huge fan of John Edward; he always taught to use tools in protecting one's space.

I have found that it is dangerous to use astral projection or do anything that makes the spirit leave the body while we are still here on earth. If the spirit leaves the body, lower energy can jump into the body and start running it.

I had an incident with the earthbound spirit of a teenage boy who felt a lot younger than his actual age and had some learning difficulties. His energy attached itself to me; I felt his presence. When I asked him why he was doing that, he said that he wanted a mum. I communicated with him and explained that it was time to let go of earth and be free of his old life. I asked his guardian angels and mine, plus the archangels Zadkiel, Michael, and Raphael, to guide him back into the spirit world so he could do his healing. I'd attracted him into my life because I loved my role as a mum and, after losing Lori, was dealing with the resulting grief.

Another time, I was doing a group meditation, and I felt the spirit of a little girl who still felt very stuck to earth. As I meditated and prayed for her, I saw Archangel Azrael and her guardian angels take her by the hand and lead her towards peace of spirit—but not before she gave me a kiss on my cheek. I felt her warmth against my face.

Sometimes when someone is in a coma or the body has suffered too much trauma, the spirit will leave the body. Also, if there is going to be an impact the spirit may leave the body prior to the impact. The spirit then does not need to take on the traumatic memories of the body, even though there may be damage to the body. It is important, once the spirit returns, that the body is still cleared of any lower energy.

Dear God and angels, thank you for always watching over our spirits.

Dependent to Independent

Sometimes within a soul family we become too dependent and intertwined. We need to learn how to become independent and follow our own dreams. That way we can come back as individuals on our own paths.

This is what happened to me when I had realised that I had lost my independence in this lifetime. One of the big lessons that I needed to learn was to be whole and independent. Once I felt full and complete, then I could join with anyone as an individual.

At first I was slowly guided to step out and push myself to expand and explore my dreams. As I healed, let go of old patterns, meditated, and used movement, I experienced a whole new level of self-assurance and confidence. I no longer fretted, and I was more peaceful and calm. I felt that all entanglements to those around me had been dropped and that I was finally a whole being. This allowed me to be more present with all those around me.

I find that doing meditation, scanning for cords wrapped around the body or linked into other people, is useful. When I do a scan of my body, I will occasionally see that someone is trying to hook into me. I visualise unravelling the rope and disengaging from the hooks.

Sometimes I have seen barbwire between me and another person, and I would need to visualise wire cutters severing the wire between myself and another.

I always call on Archangel Michael to clear any hooks or cut any rope. I then bring in the Gold Christ Light to fill me up and reset my energy.

If someone is trying to hook into my energy, I will feel dizzy or off balance, or I may feel very angry or want to swear.

I had an incident one day when all sudden all of these swear words started coming out of my mouth and I was very angry. I sat quietly and started to scan my body, and I felt a spirit within my energetic field. I asked the Archangels Michael, Azrael, and Zadkiel to come and take the spirit away from my space. As soon as the spirit lifted, I felt centred and calm once more.

The more whole I feel, the more present I can be.

Life purpose

Over the last year I have been told numerous times that every child being born now is coming in with a purpose. There is also a call to action to help Mother Earth - Gaia. We are all here to fulfil our purposes. We can no longer sit around filling up space; instead, motivation is driving every one of us forward. Our purpose is being fulfilled from a place of love and kindness towards humanity and one another.

It feels that light workers and energy healers are all being called to action, to help others heal old wounds so they can go forward with ease and guided determination.

Where people are resisting change, I am seeing bodies suffering and not wanting to complete their journeys. But once we learn to let go of the heavy weight of old suffering, our bodies can move forward much more easily.

Sometimes the fear of letting go of the old is so great, or the fear of what the new could look like stops people from wanting to let go of it. I am shown over and over that the new energy is so much lighter and happier.

It is far more painful to be stuck than to move even a little towards our joy.

Another Lower Energy

As I have seen people leaving their bodies and losing connection to their spirit through the use of alcohol and drugs, I have also seen this with some video games. I have seen first-hand that when my children play on a video gaming device they become agitated with one another and very ungrounded. They feel spacey when they come off and suffer headaches, even if it is only for a short time span.

It has been challenging as a parent when my boys come home and talk about their friends who are "all" playing a certain game, but of course I know that it may only be a few.

When I tune in to the energy of the games, I am shown that it is not only the effects of the game on the screen but also the energy of the people who have developed the game. They are not in their bodies, or they are highly medicated, or their intent is not pure. That is why the reaction by the players is so great, especially when they are children, who are so sensitive to energy.

I just knew that it wasn't a good fit for my children and was shown that it was affecting their brains. One day my youngest son came home and said that everyone was following a certain YouTuber, but when I researched it, that person's energy did not feel high. It then showed that he was being convicted of a crime and there was a petition to have his site taken down. I sat in bed that night feeling overwhelmed. I just talked to spirit, saying, "Please show me how to manoeuvre all of this with my boys." The next morning I woke to see articles on my phone detailing studies done on gaming and the effects it has on the brain and on the family unit.

I am reassured by spirit that the lessons I am teaching my children help them understand that they need to discern the energy in everything. Whether it is a television show, a video game, or a song, they need to feel the energy from it.

I ask them to feel the energy of a song. "Does it feel light and joyous, or does it feel heavy and dark?" If they answer dark or yucky, I am then guided to ask them, "Why would you allow that to come into your space, when you could have joy surrounding you?"

My children have told me that God's voice is a whisper, but evil must shout loudly to get their attention. That's true. Our spirit, our inner being, is a knowing; it is a whisper. It leads us by giving us the feeling of pure, innocent joy. Anger and fear come from outside and are loud.

It's OK to go against the grain, to be different, to be a leader.

The Energy of Entitlement Turns It to Gratitude

Over the years I have seen people acting from the state of entitlement instead of surrender and kindness.

I have had people say to me, "I will do you a favour and let you come and energy-cleanse my home"—not asking me but stating that they were doing me a kindness by letting me give up my time to do something for them.

Also, I've had people who would just keep asking me for healing sessions but offering nothing in return. During those sessions, the message that kept coming up for them was that they needed to be grateful, and they needed to give more. They needed to learn the true meaning of generosity.

Ultimately, though, the lessons came back to me. I needed to value my time and have an unwavering belief in what I offered. Occasionally the universe would put someone in my path, and I would hear "Help him" or "Help her," but the universe would always give me something in return, as an exchange of energy.

Those people who complain most about paying for a session are the ones who have lessons to learn around money. They either hold on to it too tightly or are frightened of losing it. They need to understand that it is pure energy, just like everything else, and it must flow in and out. When we surrender and trust that we are always being looked after, then the whole worry over money loosens.

We must also understand that there are light workers employed in big corporations, banks, and corporate departments, etc. who do want the best for humanity. I worked for a big corporation, and I always did the best for my clients, so it is natural to see others who are kind wanting to help.

I have learnt that it is important when making a phone call to a bank or corporate organisation to visualise the person I will be dealing with as kind, helpful, and knowledgeable and to see it as a beautiful, efficient experience in which all my needs will be met.

Occasionally I will be told by someone to ring a friend and "fix" him or her. I believe that everyone must make the first contact if he or she is guided to ask for help. I also believe that no one is broken or needs to be fixed. We are all here to accomplish our life purposes.

Other healers have told me that when their clients buy vouches for their friends, these don't get redeemed. It is more important for the people who are giving the vouchers to look at themselves and do their own healing. We cannot force others to do their healing, nor can we dictate their timing.

Sometimes the universe will put that person in front of me—I may run into them in the street—but otherwise I just send them unconditional love.

Once again, there is surrender in letting people get there in their own time, not forcing or preaching, just putting one step in front of the other on our own paths, being beacons of light and shining our way. If they are meant to see, they will. But they may get their messages another way, and we must accept that.

My children see their mummy getting on the yoga mat; they see the respect I have for my clients and how much I love doing what I do. I do not dictate or say to them the worst statement of all, "You should …" I believe that each one of my children will find his way if I am a good example of living my life on my own path.

I love and respect myself and always come from a place of love.

Paula De Francesca

Dear Universe,

Thank you for showing me how to love myself and to share this love with others.

Thank you for showing me how to take care of myself so that I may be strong and shine my light brightly.

Thank you for showing me kindness and for sending messengers to me.

May we learn to care for one another and have the understanding and patience that we are all doing our best for humanity.

Paula

Washerwoman

There are times when we go through huge learnings, to reshape us, to put us on different paths, and to clear a past life that has been activated. Sometimes we find a shadow within us that we need to heal.

I remember one Christmas Day I was standing at the kitchen sink and thinking, *This is what man-made hell feels like.* I was exhausted and feeling very much alone. All around me friends and family were laughing and smiling, but I was in pain. Physically I could not stand up anymore, mentally I was overwhelmed, and spiritually I needed my spirit team to speak louder; I felt that I couldn't hear them as clearly as I had previously.

I needed to learn that it was OK to ask for what I wanted. Why had I picked being the youngest in an older family? I had always gone along with the family decisions, not knowing that I could question any of the decisions made. With my career, for a long time I took on roles in which I wasn't in charge but was the assistant or an apprentice.

At that time, I also had many female friends who mirrored my patterns in their own lives.

From the moment I could stand, I was taught how to set and clear a table, dry dishes, fold sheets and socks, sew on a button, and cook—plus be educated and have a career.

While growing up I had the benefit of lots of adults around me. My dad would take me to tennis and school, plus he provided for the family, plus he was extremely handy and could fix anything. My mum would cook, clean, sew, work out of the home, and nurture everyone. I thought I needed to be both. I thought I needed to do everything that they did and that I needed to do it all perfectly.

I never asked for help. I would collapse with migraines but still not ask for help. As I grew up, my mother had always said, "Don't give men too many jobs, or they will get tired of you," so I was worried about the reaction if I did ask.

I was almost frightened to ask for what I needed, in case someone raised his voice or got upset with me. I certainly couldn't do confrontation. I had never seen it. My dad, a strong person, would say something and I would listen. Bosses at work would ask for something and I would do it immediately.

When my babies were small, I needed to sleep or to lie and just cuddle them and be close to them, but I attracted people in my life who called me lazy and criticised me. I attracted that because I did not believe I was worthy of honouring myself.

Instead, within a week of having a Caesarean, I would walk to and from the shops with Santino in the pusher, filled with shopping underneath to show that I was strong and that I was recovering.

This pattern continued with Enrico, when within a week of delivering him by Caesarean I was washing and mopping floors. I did not allow anyone in to help me, wanting to prove that I had this. I could do this—I was strong.

Experiencing exhaustion that I could feel right into my core, my solar plexus, and my lower back, I could no longer stand. I was in agony. I didn't just feel physically exhausted, I was mentally and emotionally depleted. I had given so much of myself for so long that I had nothing more to give, and it felt as if those around me just had their hands out taking more and more. I needed to learn to ask for help and to understand that it was not a weakness.

During this time, I was walking upstairs with a basket of laundry and leant against the wall in exhaustion and despair. I had a flash of lifetimes of walking along dusty roads carrying baskets and serving others.

I let go of grief from this lifetime and of past lifetimes.

I also needed to believe that if I did ask for help the answer would be "yes, absolutely"; I would not be shut down or thought any less of.

On this journey during which I was consumed in pain, I was shown the blessings in my actions, and I was reminded every day to look at the gratitude in my life.

When my babies woke me at night, I would see it as a blessing, as I would get to spend more time with them. I learned to change my thought patterns, and I started to feel the tightness loosening, making way for laughter and fun.

I have learnt that being independent, nourishing myself, and allowing my light to shine provide others with inspiration.

Self Is Not a Dirty Word

One thing I have learnt in my journey is setting boundaries and protecting my well-being. It was hard at first to not see this as selfish.

I have also experienced situations that have been minimised. After my miscarriages, I was told many times just to "suck it up and move on." As a child, when I would fall and get hurt, I would be told to "brush it off."

After Enrico was born and I suffered five bouts of mastitis, I was reading a copy of Louise Hay's *You Can Heal Your Life*. When I looked up the meaning of mastitis, it was all about "refusal to nourish self."

Having children brought out my strength, my voice, and ability to be an advocate for them, but when it came to me, I couldn't do it. I continued to feel bullied and weak.

The more I learnt to work with spirit, the more it built up my strength and belief that my speech and actions all came directly from spirit.

Also, a big learning was to come regarding guidance and not fear. When we act from fear, the energy is dense and heavy, but spirit is love and light.

On my eighth birthday, when my father's mother, our beloved Nonna Nina, had been hit by a train, I'd felt tremendous guilt. My dad had always watched the news, but because it was my birthday, he'd missed the news and not seen the report. My father had always been very strong and heroic. He'd delivered babies on buses and helped people. As he got older, though, he developed an aortic valve calcification in the heart, and for me it showed that holding himself tight and rigid had stopped the flow of the grief and energy leaving the body.

My dad's mum, his dad, and his brother all died at age sixty, and as *my* brother started approaching his sixtieth birthday, I noticed that I was starting to get a bit anxious. My brother became unwell, and he stopped surfing and started to post shark-watch alerts every day. I could feel fear coming from him. It hit me: maybe at some level he was frightened that there really was a sixtieth birthday curse! We all have different lessons, but my seeing this meant that there was something that needed to heal.

The three members of my family who passed over at sixty had all had different stories. My grandfather had had injuries and sickness. My grandmother had never gotten over the grief of losing her husband and had been highly medicated by doctors; I do not think she was in her body in the end. My uncle had his own illness.

I did reflect a lot on my uncle, however, as he'd always been a kind man to me. He'd been a beautiful father, always putting his hand up to coach his sons' football teams. He'd always kept himself very active, but he'd also always tried to keep the peace. Even the most reactive person around him could be calmed by his presence. He was diagnosed with bowel and stomach cancer, and it made me think that in all that smoothing out and in all that keeping of the peace, he did not get to express himself externally, instead swallowing all the strife.

His energy came through a lot while I reflected on his teachings, and this showed me that it was important to get emotions out of the body.

Movement is so beneficial. As I experienced anger and grief, I would move my body: stomping, jumping, doing anything to move that anger. For grief, I exercised my lungs and vocal cords by singing loudly. If I felt the need to yell, I would do so in the shower or into a pillow, getting it out of my body.

I remember, when I was little, going into the garage where we kept our ironing board. I saw Mum banging on the ironing board, yelling and moving. She was angry, and when she saw me, she explained that she'd needed to get the anger out of her body. I remember her shaking and banging and yelling, but as a child I didn't feel afraid. I just saw her moving energy out of her body. She wasn't directing the energy at anybody, but she knew she needed to get it out.

It's amazing how our body releases. Whenever I go for a healing, my stomach starts to rumble and gurgle, and I can feel it unclenching. Sometimes a big yawn will come, and a wave of exhaustion will wash over me as the healing process occurs. Another sign is getting goose bumps through the body and the need to go to the toilet; these are all examples of a body releasing trauma and beginning to heal.

The stronger we are, the brighter our beacon of light shines to help others.

Knowledge

The one thing the first miscarriage taught me was not to sit in the suffering. Since then, and as I entered the world of healing modalities for myself and began to do it for others, I've realised that if we ask for help it will turn up. I strongly believe that we are sent help every single day— be it a thought of encouragement from our divine, or a physical message sent, or even a person standing in front of us as a messenger.

Overprescription of medication, drugs, alcohol, and video games all push spirit out of the body and numb the sensations in our bodies, including our messages from spirit. These are the messages that tell us we are good enough. This is the encouragement that we need to hear. When we hear negative words, that is when we hurt ourselves and others, and that is not spirit.

It is so interesting how often I am guided to read a book, or research someone, or see a YouTube podcast which leads me to their teachings—and within less than twenty-four hours a client will come to me and I will be guided to talk about what I have just learnt. It is what their spirit wants for them. I am starting to understand that I really am the messenger of their spirit.

Everyone has the spirit within them, but sometimes they don't trust it or are unsure of the messages. But it is a wonderful blessing to be able to hear the spirits and to tell people their messages. It is the greatest gift, for which I am so grateful and humbled.

Sometimes I feel like a training coach, when spirit asks me to remind my client of something that he or she is being encouraged to do or change. Spirit will bring up the issue if the person has yet to change it. There will be guidance and support, and spirit will always encourage clients to be the best version of themselves and always follow their joy.

Even in my healing work, if prior to seeing my clients for the day I may be taking my children to school and I will be shown very random signs. There may be a mural being painted or a bunch of beautifully coloured birds surrounding my car or a song playing over and over, and I can just feel that this is for the client. During my sessions something will then refer me back to that sign.

Sometimes I will be guided to read a book or learn something with complete haste. I'll need to quickly learn as much as possible about something, and the very next client will need that message or reference. Once again, this constant gaining of knowledge is validated.

I am always listening to speakers and podcasts and always learning—which I love.

I remember Wayne Dyer talking about Bronnie Ware's *The Top Five Regrets of the Dying*. I had it on my bookshelf for five years before I was guided to read it. It was one of those books that I had to read because I needed to know certain material to quote to a client.

I am blessed beyond belief to be able to do this. I am extremely grateful for the ability to be a true messenger.

Sometimes I do need to use my own experiences, and I will be told the exact scenario to relate back to another. I am always guided to tell my clients exactly what I see, feel, and hear. Also, with my work this is so beneficial, as it allows any trauma to clear. It is not just about going back to where the trauma was set up but about listening to that person's spirit and giving them a chance to remove all repeated patterns and feelings of being stuck.

I am beginning to understand now why I have such a thirst for knowledge. I may need it for someone else as well as myself. I have the need to delve deeper and research. I love knowing people's stories. How did they reach their learnings? How do they teach, and how do they connect with people? What got them to the places they are today? I guess that is what I am doing with this book. I am going back to look at what got me here today and sharing it.

Spirit energy works through every one of us; we are all guided. We are part of the universe, and we are not alone. Everyone has their spirits working through them, and it is so important that we listen.

In my sessions I hear the person's spirit, and I repeat everything to them. I may be shown a scenario playing out in my mind's eye. I will also get a pain somewhere in my body if there is an event that needs to be let go. I often feel things in my solar plexus; sometimes it is a heaviness or a sick feeling if there is something I need to be alerted about. Sometimes true power and strength or excitement comes from there.

Every day I awake and ask spirit, "How can I be the best version of me today?"

Because I work with people to get their messages, I need to keep myself in a receptive state for them. I need to ensure that the messages I get are the most accurate for them.

I understand we are all trying to do our best, and I am so proud of my clients who are guided to be the best versions of themselves. I am so honoured.

Strength is asking for help; strength is looking for other alternatives; strength is believing it is OK to ask for what you need.

Spirit of a Business

From the time we were married, Rossano and I have had a business of our own. Through the years the business has grown and changed. We have been guided to adapt, move, and expand. It has taught me that businesses have their own energy too.

Each business has its own spirit, separate from its owner. It has its own needs and desires. With all the businesses that I have worked with, the spirit has wanted to serve the best way possible. It has given solutions and ideas. It wants the best for its customers and owners, and it has a voice.

The energy of the business also affects the people who work there and the people it attracts.

There is a lovely food shop near us, and every time I walk in I feel joyful. The business attracts employees who are passionate about food and are friendly and excited about being in that environment.

I have walked into other businesses and felt sadness.

I remember walking into a fruit and vegetable shop one day, one that I had never been in before. Instead of feeling the high vibration of the produce, I could smell cigarette smoke and pesticide spray. Very shortly afterwards, the business closed.

Businesses can also be affected by their location. I have done healing on businesses and found that the ground that supported it did not feel stable; it felt as if there were a big hole underneath its foundation. Once it was balanced and made secure (or in some instances moved) then the businesses could flourish and grow.

Everything is energy.

Paula De Francesca

Good Girl

I was always the good girl: helping my parents and grandparents, being around older relatives, sitting quietly, reading my books, trying to do the very best at school, and attempting not to give my parents too much trouble.

A lot of my lessons were learnt via observation. Being the youngest child in the family meant that I was still at home while my older siblings, cousins, and friends of the family were all out in the world experiencing life. I saw addiction, accidents, broken relationships, and loss, and I felt I was in the middle of it all, observing and learning. I would watch how each person would manage the situations and see the outcomes.

My older brother would always have his friends over, and I thought he was so cool talking on his CB radio and driving fast cars, which sometimes he would take me to school in. Occasionally he would challenge my parents with his actions. Seeing this, I took it upon myself not to cause any more worries for my parents, and I kept myself in check a lot of the time.

It was interesting that I later kept a lot of the trauma and growth I was experiencing, with the losses of my babies and manoeuvring through different family dynamics, hidden away from my family—from everyone. I needed to appear perfect to others but mostly to myself.

When I finally told my family of my growth and my anguish, they found it hard to deal with; instead, they needed to concentrate on positive things. They talked about me writing my book and wanted to concentrate on that. I felt that they couldn't cope when I wasn't strong or when I fell.

I remember apologising for disappointing them when I showed what I thought was weakness, not keeping everything together. Being ripped apart and then resetting ourselves in the new is what makes us who we are. The challenges and the people who block our paths and force us to look at different paths actually reaffirm our strength.

It is easier once we are fully connected to spirit and in surrender mode. We then tap into spirit's messages early upon entering difficult situations or are even guided to take different paths before things get difficult.

So many times, in my life I've thought I was travelling alone and been petrified, but I would put my foot out and walk ahead. I had to start a new school and new jobs where I knew no one. I always found strength to take that first step, but I know now that I was not alone. I always had my spirit team.

It is not about being alone. It is about *true connection*. This means being powerful instead of lonely.

I listen to my guidance early. I know that every new first step I take is supported by my spirit team.

Paula De Francesca

Synchronicity and Timing

Over the weekend my boys and I were visiting my parents. My dad told us that he had been a boy scout in the city of Luca in Italy, and he could still remember how to tie and knot the ropes. I never knew that about my dad, even though we did call him Mr Fixit. He could fix a pipe or a car, and he even sewed a bathing suit for my doll when I was little. At the exact time of my dad sharing this story of his past, Santino was doing his comprehension homework for school and picked the story he wanted to read. The last question on the activity was to research Robert Baden-Powell, a British military hero who went on to start up the Boy Scouts.

When Enrico was little and we were looking at different healing modalities, I connected with a lovely healer interstate. As we were on the phone together, she suggested, "Let's transmute any negative energy to gold healing light," and as I looked down, I saw my little boy covered in gold glitter.

I listen to another healer in the United Kingdom who occasionally will use different sprays for healing. Even though we are countries away, I will feel the coolness of the mist and smell the fragrance.

While writing this book, I was at a birthday party for one of my son's friends. As the parents stood around talking and watching the children play, one mum randomly mentioned that she donated blood on a regular basis. I was just in the process of renewing my drivers' license and had ticked the box for organ donation only that morning. It had led me to thinking whether I should give blood as well. The next day I was in a car park, and the car that pulled in right next to me had a sign saying, Give Blood Urgently. That same afternoon I noticed in front of me a different car with a sign that said, Urgent Blood Delivery. That night I was watching a TV show on my iPad that I have watched many times. Up until then it had contained no commercials, but on this occasion the one and only commercial that appeared was one asking people to donate blood. It was then that I went online and booked an appointment for my very first blood donation. The next morning I picked up my phone and saw a photo of someone who had just given blood, and it showed how the arm is bandaged after a blood donation, which I had never seen before. Two hours later, I was at the chemist when a man stood next to me with his arm wrapped in exactly the same way as that picture. Over three days I received a total of eleven messages regarding blood donation!

Finally, on the morning of day four, I found myself at the blood donation centre. I wasn't nervous of the unknown; in fact, I felt confident and self-assured. I knew I had been guided there for a reason and that everything was going to be perfect. I assured the nurse that my body would have no problems with giving blood, even though I felt that she was trying to test whether I really wanted to go through with the process. But I knew I was meant to be there. The whole process was effortless, and I was surrounded by people who felt that in their own way they were able to help another person. It was a beautiful energy to be around. A week later, I was in a state of gratitude when I received an email telling me that my blood had been used by patients in a country hospital.

Spirit, I am so excited to see where you will guide me next.

Paula De Francesca

Genetic Trauma

As I have been working more and more with clients, I've realised how much our genetic imprint can affect us. We pick the parents who have lessons for us and the lineage they carry.

There was an incident one day while my grandmother was in a nursing home: the nurse said that she had slapped another patient. When we asked my grandmother, she said that the lady reminded her of her mother-in-law, who had not been very nice to my grandmother. My grandmother's mother-in-law had put needles in my grandmothers' bed and ordered her around. As she'd been reflecting on her life, this trauma had come up, and she'd felt the need to defend herself, since she hadn't been able to the last time and had had to endure the treatment. My grandmother said that the lady she had slapped looked like her mother-in-law.

I had picked two parents who'd had to flee their homes and their birth country as children due to the war. My father had had his house bombed. His mum had been cooking in the kitchen when a bomb had come through the roof. His mum, brother, and my dad had had to hide under the table as smoke enveloped them. They then had been rescued by the fire brigade.

My father's father had been in the navy during the Second World War and had to swim to shore after the ship he was on was torpedoed.

My mother's family had been brought up in a village, but once again due to the war, my mother had had to flee her home with her mother and younger brother in preparation for leaving on a ship to Australia. She was reunited with her father, who had been away at war, just before they left for Australia.

My parents met in the refugee camp just before they boarded the ship that would commence their voyage to Australia with their respective families.

When they arrived in Australia, they were housed in refugee camps before they were sent off to work. All the men were sent to farms to help and earn enough money to pay off their voyage and settle their family in Adelaide.

My grandmother made a lot of good friends during this time, and they formed their own new community. All these people created their own new families to help fill the void of the families they'd lost or left behind.

The friends they made in the camp or on the boat stayed with them until they became old. Even after my grandmother passed away, my mother continued to stay in contact with these friends and their families. These were lifelong friendships built in a challenging situation, which allowed all of them to grow and push themselves. They were all given the opportunity to reinvent themselves. There was a feeling of independence, as so many people had been displaced or left with only a few members of their families.

Some people never were able to settle into this new country. The pull of their home was too strong, and they had to go back to Italy, but my grandfather would always say, "Australia number one." He loved the climate and the lifestyle. I think he loved the peace after being in the war with many active tours of duty in Africa and Europe. He wasn't made for fighting, and the thought of having to go back to the front line made him take drastic action. He blew his own thumb off so that he would be kept in an Italian hospital. In Australia he found joy in music and always looked for peace.

Even in the final week of his life, after he had suffered a stroke, we came out of the hospital lift and found him in the hallway, dancing to his radio. A few days later another stroke caused his spirit to leave his body. That was on Sunday, 18 August 1991.

Paula De Francesca

Lessons

Why are some people so often present when others pass away? My uncle, such an unselfish man, sent his family home so he could pass away quietly and without fuss after carrying cancer in his body. He chose to pass over on June 13, the feast day of St Anthony of Padova, the saint his mother had such faith in.

I have friends who have been present with so many of their relatives as they passed over. They sit by their beds, hold their hands until their last breath has been taken, and provide comfort. It always makes me wonder why some people would experience that so many times.

I sometimes reflect on the way people die. Some people take a long time for their body to officially power down; they want their families close with every breath. It feels that they are frightened of leaving their families; they may not want to leave them alone. Some may have a crisis of conscience in that moment, thinking that they will have to look at things that they have been putting off.

I have been shown that we have agreements in place about our time on earth *before* we come into our physical bodies. Some who come in for shorter lives remember this agreement and come in with such purpose and drive. They know that they only have a limited time on earth to achieve what they've agreed to do in this lifetime. There is extreme comfort in this for me when I realise that these children and youth already know that there is limited physical time to help those around them.

Growing up, I saw people who did not choose to live their lives to their full purpose; they were so angry and blamed those around them for troubles in their lives. They caused a lot of hurt, and their deaths were very long. They would be immobile in the last years of their life, and there would be hardly any connection between their physical bodies and spirit.

I remember my mum telling me that when my uncle passed away, she had been called to come to the hospital. Even though my uncle had already passed, his hands were warm, and both Mum and Dad noticed a whirring sound above them and could see a mist. Even though they were in shock, they felt comforted. My dad told me that my uncle had always had a strong faith, especially through his childhood and as he had become sick he would ask my dad to pray with him. He died fully at peace, knowing that he had lived his life for his family and inspired all to look for the good in those around them.

My mum said that this was only the second time she had seen my dad cry; the other was when his mother had passed away.

I talk to my boys about this; I encourage them to cry and let out their feelings. My dad always felt the need to be the strong one. Being the eldest son, his brother being a lot younger, and his dad at war, my dad had to step up. He is always the leader in any situation, directing and pulling people together. Even his stature is tall and strong, and his voice is loud. My mum always teases my dad, telling him he can't whisper. He is a Capricorn, which is why he likes order. He is highly reflective, though, and will continue to journal to this day, recalling instances in his life and offering pearls of wisdom and guidance.

"Always surround yourself with positive people, Paula," he tells me.

He always reminds me how strong I am.

When I was growing up, it was beautiful to see Mum and Dad's love for one another. They have always been very considerate of one another. They exchange love notes or leave a token of a flower or teddy bear on a pillow. My dad always says how beautiful my mum is. I love the saying "When you first fall in love, you hold hands, as you want to be close, and as you get older and frailer, you hold hands to support one another."

Yes, Mum and Dad may bicker, but they always laugh it off. Neither of them holds grudges and never did the silent treatment. They were rarely unwell, but the one time my dad fainted, due to heat exhaustion, he pulled me to one side and said, "Make sure you always look out for your mother." He was the most vulnerable I had ever seen him in that moment.

Dad has always been very mobile. He played tennis with me, we always went to the beach, and while my boys were growing up he was there as well, swimming out into the ocean with them. Even in his eighties, he still has phenomenal driving skills and quick reflexes. He is such an inspiration for me to ensure I keep my fitness and strength, so I can be mobile and active both physically and mentally.

Mum and Dad always shared the love of music and dance. Even now, when I pop in I can find them dancing in the kitchen to the tunes of the Italian radio.

They do life well. They have a passion for food, especially the produce grown and handpicked from their garden. Their house is filled with music, writing, and movement. They exhibit a passion for life and great unconditional love for their children and grandchildren.

It is interesting, though, that as I ask for more evidence of motivation in my life and as I work on strengthening my body, this reflection is done through my parents, both in their eighties and still being a pinnacle of motivation. I get great joy in seeing Dad as he hijacks my children's scooters and rides them around his backyard or Mum catching a tennis ball with such accuracy and bowling it back like a professional.

Paula De Francesca

Past Lives

I have had to address past lives, karma and contractual agreements for my own learnings and for my family. I have had past lives where I experienced famine, lack, and war, and these needed to be cleared because they have affected my belief pattern in this lifetime.

I had an incident when I pulled back curtains in my home—and had a very strong vision of a past life, when I was a maid drawing curtains back for a very grand lady. I had a very servile attitude, not one of equality but of putting others on a pedestal. This belief from the past was affecting my life in the present.

Meditation is a wonderful thing for going back to a past life. It is important to clear any trauma and reset the emotion. By going back to the original set-up of the trauma, one can clear it for the initial past life and any future patterns.

We need to believe that we are most valuable and are here to do something special on this earth—and that means all of us.

Especially in the current time, the people coming onto this planet have very strong life paths and are here for a purpose. People who have reincarnated numerous times before are not as quick to come back this time, unless they have a very distinct life purpose.

Everyday living out of your life purpose, even though it may seem the most miniscule thing, may be just the thing you need that day to guide you along your path.

Some days the activities are going to seem bigger than others.

Some days it does feel that mountains have been moved.

Some days it really is as simple as saying a prayer.

It is important to start your day right, to have an intent, to always have gratitude, and to pray,

"God, please show me what I need to do today to walk my life path" and then be open to being shown.

I have a knowing and a belief that we do have a purpose for being on this planet currently—all of us—but it's not about dictating to others. Sometimes it's in the journey, in finding what is in the twists and turns, that gets us to our life paths. The journey connects us with others. Sometimes we need to meet the right teacher at the right time to trigger something, so we then get the learning and the expansion.

It is important to keep a high vibrational state and not binge eat or drink to stuff down our emotions. We must keep our guidance coming through as clearly as possible.

The journey on our life paths is about following the joy.

From the baby being born onto this earth we learn to follow our joy.

Listening to beautiful music gives us joy; dancing and moving gives us joy; reading, wonder, and discovery all follow the joy that leads us to our next step, then our next step, and then our next step.

We are presented with teachers that are put into our paths. They may not look like traditional teachers in school; they could be practitioners or colleagues.

We are guided to look for our reaction in the company of friends or other people. What are our triggers? Where do we feel most at home and face least resistance?

There is a difference, though, I am guided to say, between joy and physical pleasure. Self-gratifying pleasure may not provide the joy that keeps us on our life paths. Self-gratification can be selfish and can lead to pain and addiction. It can alienate people; it is about external fulfilment of self and very much in the ego mindset. It is about competition and wanting to take from others.

Believing that we are not good enough, or always comparing ourselves to others, or looking outside of ourselves to see if we measure up will see us always chasing something external, looking for external things to fill us up.

Whereas, the joy of being on our life path is in connecting with others, kindness to self and others, and of gratitude and blessings.

Following our joy provides no resistance, no fear or worry. It is a natural flow of waves of happiness or tingles through our bodies.

If I am guided, then I believe and I know that everything for that next step is already there, and so it goes in every step … every step … every step.

Synchronicity means things just turning up easily, without us having to push, argue, fight, or justify. It will just naturally flow, especially as we get into the practice of it in every moment of every day.

There's a contrast in feeling the tightness versus the ease, and sometimes we set ourselves up to feel that discomfort in order to spur us to change direction.

We are filled from within, with the light of our spirit.

Call of Home

Certain places just feel comfortable and homey. It's possible we have had lifetimes there or maybe these are genetic memories.

We also long for certain places; it's not just the joy of having a holiday. It goes deeper.

Certain places have deep connections with people, and they find themselves driven back to those homes. They may not have ever visited a place, but when they go there they get a feeling of being at home.

I have found this feeling in Australia and Italy, so far. When I am home in Australia, it feels right; I feel welcome and at ease. But I have also felt the pull of Italy through the years. I believe that because of my genetic memory with my parents, there is an underlying call to their home. Even the first time I went to Italy, when I was ten, it just felt right, and every time I've returned since I have just felt supported.

I look forward to being guided to homes that welcome me.

Paula De Francesca

Gratitude

This book would not be complete unless I dedicated it to gratitude. Gratitude helps me in every situation.

When I help my clients, I thank spirit that I am able to be their messenger.

With my family, I thank spirit for the beautiful guidance I receive and which I can share with my boys.

Every moment of every day and everywhere I look, I see things to be grateful for. It may be the restful sleep I experienced and thanking my pillow and bed for their comfort. It may be the smile from the shop assistant. It may be a wave from a friend.

There are days when I will write a list of all the things that I am grateful for. Other days I will bring to the forefront of my mind all the beauty I see. I will say thank you silently, or in a whisper, or aloud, or I will shout it with enthusiasm and gusto.

I give gratitude to the teachers in my children's lives. I give gratitude to the guides who appear before me. I give gratitude to my clients who trust me to be the messenger of their spirit. I give gratitude to all my family members and friends who reflect their love back to me.

I give gratitude to all the experiences and learnings and I am grateful that I am able to recognise them as blessings.

I give gratitude that I am able to share my love with others and to receive such beautiful love back.

I give gratitude for my husband, and friends, and family, who hold such a sacred space to allow me to process my feelings and thoughts and create beliefs to affirm that we are all such truly magnificent beings.

I give gratitude for things I can see, touch, feel, and smell, and I give gratitude to things I know are always around me even though I may not physically experience them.

I give gratitude for faith, the ability to know that I am always supported and that I can jump even when I can't see the net catching me. I give gratitude to my spirit team, for all my learnings and the ability to help others.

I give gratitude for things I have yet to experience but know that I am supported and guided in every step.

The more in the space of gratitude I am, the more the universe gives me things to be grateful about.

References

Books:-

Dyer, Wayne W Dr, *Getting in the Gap, United States, Hay House Inc, 2003*

Hay, Louise L, *You Can Heal Your Life, United States, Hay House Inc, 1984*

Hay, Louse L, *Mirror Work: 21 Days to Heal Your Life, United States, Hay House Inc, 2016*

Solter, Aletha, *The Aware Baby, United States, Shining Star Press, 2001*

Valentine, Radleigh, *How to Be Your Own Genie, United States, Hay House Inc, 2017*

Virtue, Doreen, Mary Queen of Angels Oracle Cards, *United States, Hay House Inc, 2012*

Ware, Bronnie, *The Top Five Regrets of the Dying, United States, Hay House Inc, 2012*

Training:-

Wipfler, Patty, Hand in Hand Instructor Certification Program

Hay, Louse L, Loving Yourself, 21 Days to improved Self-Esteem and Mirror Work

Linn, Denise, Method for Transformation Certified Clutter Coach

Richards, Steve, Holographic Kinetics, An Advanced Aboriginal Healing Modality.

Other References:-

John Edward, *Crossing Over* television program

Abraham Hicks, various podcasts

Cambridge Dictionary – www.dictionary.cambridge.org

Songs:-

Katrina and the Waves - Walking on Sunshine, released 1983

Eurythmics - There Must Be an Angel, released 1985

Lucybell – Angel, released 2004

Online Presence

My website

http://helpingparents.com.au

Social Media

Facebook
https://www.facebook.com/Helping-Parents-375048372914554/?ref=aymt_homepage_
panel&eid=ARDkrgp_PFBvMyDpQKp8kBPG6QycPGxAmUTeKoqeZMJWTinnmvG
kRKj4rapY3AmApqsG-ES6pRxdoH4q

You Tube Channel
https://www.youtube.com/watch?v=XVq6RP8JM_A

Qualifications

Hand in Hand Parenting Instructor
Holographic Kinetics Practitioner
Space Clearer
Spiritual Healer
Certified Angel Intuitive
Clutter Coach
Certified Crystal Reader
Certified Assertiveness Coach
Certified Flower Therapy Healer
Member of the International Institute for Complementary Therapists

Acknowledgements

I acknowledge with gratitude my beautiful soul family here on earth and in spirit. Thank you for the blessings and teachings.

I thank my wonderful husband, who encourages me to grow and evolve and who listens.

To my beautiful babies in spirit form: you have taught me so much, and I am grateful for our connection. Thank you for choosing me, my darlings.

To my two beautiful sons: thank you for your cuddles, your kisses, and your love. Thank you for every learning and for your acts of pure surrender.

To the readers of this book: I hope that by sharing these words I am providing you with teachings and healings you can use. I hope that at least one sentence can provide you with the comfort you need and the reassurance that you are not alone on earth. I thank you for sharing in my vulnerability.

To spirit: thank you. I am one with you, I feel you, I connect with you, I surrender.

Author Biography

Paula De Francesca is a wife and a mum of two beautiful boys, who lives in Adelaide, South Australia. After leaving the corporate world behind to have children, Paula felt guided to change old patterns and to grow. As she experienced multiple miscarriages and grief, each milestone of parenting and loss enabled her to grow, expand, and learn.

Paula is now a spiritual messenger, guiding others to let go of grief and be the best versions of themselves, free of heaviness and old patterns.

Paula lives every day in true surrender, and with guidance of her spirit team, she teaches her children to do the same.

Paula continues to be open to the lessons from the universe. She knows that she is always truly supported with every step of her life path.

Every day she wakes up and says, "Show me the beautiful miracles of today," and she ends every day in deep gratitude and appreciation of this world and the support she has received.

Notes

Printed in the United States
By Bookmasters